Winning the War Over What-ifs:

A Practical Guide to Living Empowered

Billie Corley

Unless otherwise noted, Scripture quotations used in this book are from *The Holy Bible*, King James Version (KJV). © 1973, 1978, 1984, 2011 International Bible Society. Used by permission of Zondervan Bible Publishers.

Other Scripture references are from the following sources:
New King James Version (NKJV), ©1979, 1980, 1982, Thomas Nelson, Inc.
Amplified® Bible (AMP), Copyright © 2015 by The Lockman Foundation. Used by permission. lockman.org,
Amplified® Bible, Classic Edition (AMPC), Copyright © 1954, 1958, 1962, 1964, 1965, 1987 by The Lockman Foundation Used by permission. lockman.org.
The Living Bible (TLB), copyright © 1971 by Tyndale House Foundation. Used by permission of Tyndale House Publishers, Carol Stream, Illinois 60188. All rights reserved.
Good News Translation in Today's English Version (GNT) - Second Edition Copyright © 1992 by American Bible Society. Used by Permission.

Winning the War Over What-ifs: A Practical Guide to Living Empowered, Billie Corley.
Issued in electronic and paperback formats
Paperback ISBN: 979-8-9897467-7-4
E-book ISBN: 979-8-9897467-8-1
LCCN: 2025919702
First Edition

Publisher: Dressed in Love Press, LLC
www.drkatherinehayes.com
Cover Designer: Katherine Hutchinson-Hayes
Book Interior Designer: Jenifer Jennings
Printed in the United States of America

To my soulmate, Ben,

Thank you for your support, encouragement, patience, and the sacrifices you made as I wrote this book. May God abundantly bless you for all you have done for me. I love you bunches and bunches and bunches and bunches.

Table of Contents

Foreword

Several years ago, I had the pleasure of meeting Billie Corley at a conference where she invited me to serve as her editor. From the very beginning, I was struck by her passion, her love for people, and her remarkable gift for weaving words with purpose and conviction.

It became clear to me that Billie carried a unique calling—to ignite the hearts of women and to draw them closer to Jesus Christ.

Winning the War Over What-ifs is not just another book; it is the culmination of Billie's life work. These pages reflect her passionate desire to encourage women to step out of fear and uncertainty and into a life empowered by faith. Her writing offers both testimony and invitation—drawing readers into deeper trust in God while equipping them with practical truth for victorious living.

As you journey through this book, you will sense the depth of Billie's heart, her devotion to Christ, and her genuine desire to see others flourish in Him. This work is filled with encouragement, wisdom, and biblical insights that will stir your spirit, renew your hope, and remind you that in Christ, victory over life's 'what-ifs' is always possible. It is with great joy and honor that I commend this book to you.

May Billie's words bless you richly, as they have blessed me.

—Dr. Katherine Hutchinson-Hayes

Introduction

"My case is urgent, and I do not see how I am to be delivered, but that is no business of mine. He who makes the promise will find ways and means of keeping it. It is mine to obey His commands; it is not mine to direct His counsel. I am His servant, not His solicitor. I call upon Him, and He will deliver me."[1]

–C. H. Spurgeon

Gaining victory over the *what-ifs* demands fully surrendering to God's ways, total dependence upon His guidance, sensitivity to the leadership of the Holy Spirit, unlimited trust, and giving more than you realized you had to offer. You won't find the phrase *What-if Moment* in a dictionary. Inspiration came to write this book for two reasons. One came while reading biblical stories and imagining choices, actions, and reactions. For instance, consider Shadrach, Meshach, and Abednego, the three Hebrew children, who were forced to choose between bowing to the king's image or being thrown into a fiery furnace (Daniel 3).

While reading their story, I wondered, *what if* they opted to blend in with the crowd to avoid the furnace and bowed to the king's image? The storyline would have been different. King Nebuchadnezzar would have missed seeing the pre-incarnate Jesus with the three Hebrew children in the fire. "He answered and said, Lo, I see four men loose, walking in the midst of the fire, and they have no hurt; and the form of the fourth is like the Son of God" (Daniel 3:25). Another inspiration for writing this book came from a passage I read in Mrs. Charles E. Cowman's book, *Streams in the Desert*. "Every hard duty that lies in your path that you would rather not do, that it will cost you pain and struggle or sore effort to do, has a blessing in it. Not to do it, at whatever cost, is to miss a blessing."[2] I put Mrs. Cowman's words on my wall as a reminder that there's a blessing in what-if moments. We all have a choice: stop short and miss the blessing or press forward and receive it. The choice is ours.

Winning the War over What-ifs isn't "what we do," but what we allow God's power to do through us. I titled every chapter with "Empowered" as a constant reminder that only in His power are we victorious. God manifests His power through our what-if moments, empowering us to triumph over them. Within this book, I share my challenges and stories from the Old and New Testament saints. You'll be inspired as you read about how God provided a path when none existed and how He revealed His wonderworking, grace-filled, strength-bestowing nature above our concerns.

God is omnipotent, all-knowing, and omnipresent. He's "...Alpha, Omega, the beginning and the ending...which was, and which is to come, the Almighty" (Revelation 1:8). Throughout this book, it will be apparent that God is the Supreme Ruler. Our what-if moments are divine opportunities for God to teach us about not only Himself, but who we are in Him.

Our what-if moments do not surprise God. From the moment of creation, God set a detailed plan in motion. Scripture after scripture confirms that God not only created the universe but also continually controls every aspect as His purpose is accomplished. What-ifs are a setup for God's purpose to be fulfilled. Sometimes our path appears to lead us away from God's purpose. However, if we follow God's leadership as He orders our steps, we'll discover that even the unexpected detours were a part of the journey. For example, God ordained Joseph to be ruler of Egypt, "to save much people alive" (Genesis 50:20). Although Joseph's what-if moment when his brothers threw him into the pit appeared to be out of order according to God's plan, it was God's chosen path from the pasture where he shepherded sheep to the palace where God would use him to save the nation of Israel.

What-ifs are of God's choosing. Through divine guidance, God will lead us from where we are to where we're meant to be. For example, in the book of Ruth, Naomi was in Moab. Through the change in her circumstances, losing her husband and sons and a famine, God led Naomi to Bethlehem-Judah, the place where her daughter-in-law, Ruth, would meet and marry Boaz and become a part of the lineage of Christ. This story shows that often, there must be a leaving before arriving at God's appointed place (Matthew 1:6).

At the what-ifs, impassable becomes passable. Following their miraculous escape from the Egyptians, the Israelites' what-if moment included the enemy chasing them and the Red Sea blocking their path. Without a boat or bridge, how were they supposed to escape? However, God held the waters back while the Israelites passed over to the other side.

> "And it came between the camp of the Egyptians and the camp of Israel; and it was a cloud and darkness to them, but it gave light by night to these: so that the one came not near the other all the night. And Moses stretched out his hand over the sea; and the LORD caused the sea to go back by a strong east wind all that night, and made the sea dry land, and the waters were divided." (Exodus 14:20-21)

The what-ifs are where the enemy is defeated, and God is glorified. "And Israel saw that great work which the Lord did upon the Egyptians: and the people feared the Lord, and believed the Lord, and his servant Moses" (Exodus 14:31). What-if moments are the safest place to be because God is there. You'll discover throughout the chapters of this book that winning the war over *what-ifs* will require risk-taking, quick decisions, faith, and self-denial. You'll encounter moments of tears, prayers without ceasing, discouragement, depression, and a determination to withstand the strain.

Empowerment comes as we place our faith in God's plans since:

- God's plans are SOLID.
- God's plans are INTENTIONAL.
- God's plans are UNSTOPPABLE.
- God's plans are EXACT.
- God's plans are a TESTIMONY of His greatness.
- God's plans are for us to SUCCEED.

Empowerment to flourish in the what-if moments results from:

- Placing absolute trust in God's plan even when it makes little sense.
- A willingness to go through to the other side.
- Expecting and preparing for the battle.

Often, Satan uses *what-if* scenarios as an attempt to impede God's plan. Many what-if moments came up as I wrote this book. For instance, two days after signing the contract for my book, I became extremely sick.

Throughout these past months, I have fought fatigue and brain fog. My printer died. Our home was struck by lightning, causing damage that needed repairs and loss of the internet (which I heavily relied upon). We even had to call the fire department because of a burning wire smell. Throughout my what-if moments, God reminded me that "power belongeth unto Him" (Psalm 62:11).

The stories and testimonies in this book are designed to recharge your spiritual tank with faith, joy, love, and trust. Fresh energy will rise in your spirit as you read testimony after testimony of God's greatness. My goal is to keep us motivated, stirred up, "to incite us to action" so we can live fully charged before a world without Christ.

By embracing a winning attitude, you'll be continually inspired by those who seized their what-if moment and rose. Likewise, you'll learn to act decisively, elevating your confidence and ability to win the war over your what-ifs.

"Father, I thank You for each person reading this book. Thank You for the gift of their time as they read Your message. I pray the truths You have given me will strengthen their faith and give them a hunger and thirst for more of You in their daily walk. May you use the words of this book to renew hope and bring refreshment to their spirit. Lord, please confirm You're with them every step of their journey and they're empowered with Your unlimited power. Thank you for the victory over the *what-ifs*. May You be glorified. Thank You, Lord, for Your faithfulness, helping me overcome in my what-if moment*s*. You have been so good to me. May all that is written on the pages of this book glorify your magnificent Name. To God be the glory, great and mighty things He has done. In Jesus' Name, Amen."

All for His glory,
Billie

Chapter 1
Empowered by Hope

"Trials teach us what we are; they dig up the
soil and let us see what we are made of."[3]
–Charles Spurgeon

Do you have a favorite bible story you love to read repeatedly? I have several examples, such as the verses from Ezekiel 37, where God instructed Israel's prophet Ezekiel to prophesy over a valley filled with dry bones. "So I prophesied as I was commanded: and as I prophesied, there was a noise, and behold a shaking, and the bones came together, bone to *his* bone" (Ezekiel 37:7).

Did you catch "bones came together, bone to his bone?" God is meticulous. Bones weren't randomly connected; they came together, bone to bone. But wait, it gets even better! After the bones connected, Ezekiel breathed breath into them. The bones not only came back to life but were immediately transformed into a massive army. When the breath of life breathed upon the slain, "they lived, and stood up upon their feet, an exceeding great army" (Ezekiel 37:10). They transitioned from "lifeless and powerless to alive and powerful." How cool is that? Occasionally, our what-ifs seem impossible, but with God, nothing is impossible. Not even a graveyard filled with parched bones.

Would you like to visit the graveyard with me so we can take a closer look? Be warned, the scene is quite desolate on arrival. Where a massive army once was, now lies an enormous heap of bones. All one can perceive is defeat, death, and devastation—a place of no hope. There's no need to despair. Although it appears the bones' chance of recovery has vanished, the sovereignty of God still reigns. Even the driest bones can be restored to new life. Your courage will soar as you see IM-possible become HIMpossible.[4]

There are three challenges to observe in this scenario.

- **A somber image**: The once vibrant land was desolate and lifeless. A place that was once filled with sound is now silent as death has taken over (Ezekiel 37:1-2).

- **A staggering question:** As Ezekiel looked at the lifeless bones, God interrupted his thoughts with a strange question, "Son of Man, can these bones live?" (Ezekiel 37:3). From man's point of view, death had won, leaving no hope of life. Yet, Ezekiel viewed the bone's plight through God's eyes and replied, "O Lord God, thou knowest."

- **A startling command:** Not only did God ask a staggering question, but He also shocked Ezekiel with an astonishing command: Preach to the bones! What? Their flesh had disintegrated. The ears were gone! How could God expect the dry bones to hear His Word? Because God's Word is powerful enough to penetrate the joints and marrow (Ezekiel 37:4-5).

Two powerful aspects of this scenario ultimately defeat each challenge.

- **Nothing can stop God's Word from carrying out that which He pleases:** "The Word of God is living and powerful, and sharper than any two-edged sword, piercing even to the dividing asunder of soul and spirit, and of the joints and marrow...." (Hebrews 4:12). "So shall my word be that goeth forth out of my mouth: it shall not return unto me void, but it shall accomplish that which I please, and it shall prosper in the thing whereto I sent it" (Isaiah 55:11).

- **The Word of God is the bones' sole hope for living:** "Most assuredly, I say to you, he who hears My word and believes in Him who sent Me has everlasting life, and shall not come into judgment, but has passed from death into life" (John 5:24).

Several responses and actions took place, which caused the "impossible" to become "possible."

- **A simple act of obedience:** So, Ezekiel prophesied as he was commanded. Sometimes God directs us to do something beyond our comprehension. Obedience to God's commands open doors for His authority to rule. Notice Ezekiel's response to God's command, "So I prophesied as I was commanded and as I prophesied, there was a noise, and behold a shaking, and the bones came together, bone to his bone" (Ezekiel 37:7). What if Ezekiel had not been obedient? There would have been no noise nor shaking, and the valley of no hope would have remained hopeless. Do you want victory over your what-if moment? Then, obey God and watch the Almighty revive that which was once dead come to life.

- **The slain and scattered bones arose, came together, and formed a mighty army**: What we regard as a graveyard, God envisions an army in the making (Ezekiel 37:10).

- **That which was dead came to life:** Under God's authority, death and decay are powerless (Ez 37:13).

- **The Valley of NO HOPE was transformed into the Valley of HOPE:** When the great I AM exerts His authority, hopelessness must flee (Ez 37:12-14).

- **A spectacular outcome:** When God performs miracles, there is no doubt about who has spoken, "…then shall ye know that I the LORD have spoken it, and performed it, saith the LORD" (Ezekiel 37:14). It doesn't matter how critical your what-if moment is; with God, the outcome is beyond anything you can imagine.

I don't know the circumstances involved in your *what-if*. Or if you, like the nation of Israel, regard all hopes as lost (Ezekiel 37:11). Be confident, God is the Supreme Ruler. His Authority governs all things, and He is in control. Embrace hope. When your adversary whispers, "No hope," draw your weapon, hold up your shield of faith as you fearlessly declare, "It is written." Remind your enemy of God's promise. "And [I] shall put my spirit in you, and ye shall live, and I shall place you in your own land: then shall ye know that I the LORD have spoken it, and performed it, saith the LORD" (Ezekiel 37:14).

Before considering your what-if moment as hopeless, wait for the seed of hope to sprout and watch hope come alive as the God of hope, "…fill you with all joy and peace in believing, that ye may abound in hope" (Romans 15:13).

Seeds of Hope

Are you in the pit of despair with no hope in sight?
Has fear fueled your mind, causing you to fright?
When the days appear hopeless and troubles abound,
Remember, a flower's journey starts in the ground.
Just as the seed's life begins in dark, damp soil,
God is growing you during these days of toil.
As you wait and watch for the sprout,
Resist the temptation to worry and doubt.
Although the process is slow and full of strife,
Don't forget, only planted seeds develop into new life.
Your bouquet has a purpose and will be assembled in
God's perfect time.
Trust in knowing that God's ways are always sublime!
Even though for a while you're surrounded by
darkness and gloom,
In the end, God's flawless design will astonishingly
emerge and bloom.
Whereas the journey is challenging, never lose hope.
As the seed survived, God will help you cope.
Therefore, be encouraged, God is unfolding your
story.
So that when your buds blossom out, they'll bring
Him glory!

—Billie Corley

Empowerment through Hope Battle Plan:

Have you ever felt spiritually dry, as if your life lacks purpose or vitality? When these moments come, do you remember the promise of God's Living Water—the eternal source of hope and renewal? Reflect on John 4:14, where Jesus speaks of a well that forever satisfies our deepest thirst. Are you thirsty for renewal? Are you open to rehydrating your soul with the invigorating waters of His grace?

Take time today to ask yourself: How can I invite God's hope into my dry moments?

What steps can I take to immerse myself more deeply in His Word and His promises? Remember, just as physical hydration restores our body, hope in God's Word replenishes our spirit.

Let's commit to seeking His Living Water daily. Reach out, pray, open the Bible, and allow the hope of Christ to empower you anew. How will you embrace hope today?

Chapter 2
Empowered to Live Fully Charged

"You cannot kindle a fire in any other heart
until it is burning within your own."[5]
—Ralph Waldo Emerson

Do you write in a journal? Years ago, I began journaling and discovered it was beneficial for expressing my thoughts on paper. I especially enjoy going back and reading what I have written. I chuckled while going through old journals. I often called on God to assist me in realigning my diet and improving my time management skills so I could be more productive and avoid wasting time. Day after day, I recorded the things I wanted to do, but didn't do, and the things I did that I didn't want to do. Does this sound familiar? Paul the apostle had similar struggles. "I know that good does not live in me—that is, in my human nature. For even though the desire to do good is in me, I am not able to do it. I don't do the good I want to do; instead,

I do the evil that I do not want to do" (Romans 7:18-19 GNT).

James 1:25 instructs the Christian to "…be ye doers of the word, and not hearers only, deceiving your own selves." I have no problem living out Romans 7:18-19. Like Paul, I wonder who can rescue me; thanks be to God, through Christ Jesus I am freed from sin. "What an unhappy man I am! Who will rescue me from this body that is taking me to death? Thanks be to God, who does this through our Lord Jesus Christ" (Romans 7:24-25 GNT).

Are you like me and need a good shake from the Lord to wake up the slumbering spirit? Why do we find it challenging to "live fully charged?" Most of us know what it means to fall into a spiritual slump. There's hope on the horizon as we learn how to "get real and find the zeal." As we embrace that God has empowered us to do great things for Him. From time to time, life may knock us down. But it's not how many times we fall, it's the getting back up that counts. Living empowered means, it's time to rise up, wise up, buck up, cheer up, and never give up. It's a reminder to tap into the power that's within and commit not to live as a spiritual pauper but live a life full of the goodness of God.

Living fully charged in our *what-ifs* requires a healthy dose of spiritual supplements. Sluggishness is defined as "averse to activity or exertion. Or slow to respond (as to stimulation or treatment). It's markedly slow in movement, flow, or growth."[6] The opposite of sluggishness, zealous, is "marked by fervent devotion for a person, a cause, or an ideal: filled with or characterized by zeal."[7]

When we feel spiritually sluggish, it means the Holy Spirit isn't flowing freely within our spirit. Just like a clogged pipe, if the condition isn't corrected, we'll have a huge plumbing bill. Apathy will override the Christian's fervor—provoking doubt, discouragement, and despair. Our spiritual energy will be zapped, and thoughts of quitting will override the desire to finish our course.

According to an article written by Jon Bloom, we see an excellent illustration that defines the term spiritually sluggish.

"Spiritual sluggishness is a manifestation of unbelief. It's a sign that there's something about God that we doubt, and it's draining our hope, which means it's draining our energy and drive. We're not giving it all we have because we doubt it's worth the effort. Sluggishness in a runner signals danger to a coach. Something isn't right. Something is causing ambivalence, draining confidence. The runner is losing heart. Half-hearted running is a forerunner to quitting."[8]

Bloom demonstrates that being half-hearted in sports is the same as being unenthusiastic in our walk with Christ. Our spiritual sluggishness signals danger to God that we're on the verge of quitting. As Christians, we're to live zealously before God and monitor closely any thoughts of quitting. We're to push past the obstacles and tap into supernatural strength so we can run the race before us.

Are you exercising your spiritual gift? First Corinthians urges Christians to seek zealously spiritual gifts that build up the church (1 Corinthians 14:12). Jesus gave Himself for us so that "he might redeem us from all iniquity, and purify unto himself a peculiar people, zealous of good works" (Titus 2:14). How can we live fully charged in the what-if moments? I once saw an advertisement with the motto, "Live Fully Charged." My first thought was yes! If we're zealous of the LORD, our faith will be fully charged.

In the book of Luke, we see an excellent example of what it means to live fully charged—through four men's what-if moments. Nothing could stop them from achieving their goal—bringing their friend to Jesus.

In the fifth chapter of Luke, Jesus teaches in a crowded room, and the power of Christ is present to heal. Four men, eager to help their paralyzed friend, looked for a way to get him to Jesus. But a massive crowd blocked their path. So, they went with Plan B — "Lower him down through the roof!" (I often wondered which of the four men came up with the idea … "If we can't get him through, we'll go up and get him down." For one, that person exemplified zealousness to the fullest.) Since the crowds blocked their path, they headed to the roof with their paralyzed friend in tow.

After creating a hole big enough for their friend and his bed, Jesus looks up and sees them. There was no reference regarding the unusual entry, just that "…when Jesus saw their faith, He said unto him, 'Man, thy sins are forgiven of thee'" (Luke 5:20).

What impressed Jesus the most? Was it because the friends didn't allow the crowded room to stop them? Or that they would even think of bringing their friend down through the roof? It was their faith. An important lesson to remember is that the four men didn't place their faith in getting their friend to Jesus. They put their trust in Jesus and His ability to heal their friend. Their belief (not their actions) stirred Jesus' heart and aroused a response. On the contrary, the scribes and Pharisees weren't the least bit impressed. In fact, they were baffled, causing them to ask—

> "…who can forgive sins, but God alone? But when Jesus perceived their thoughts, He answering said unto them, "What think ye in your hearts? Whether is easier, to say, Thy sins be forgiven thee; or to say, Rise up and walk? But that ye may know that the Son of man hath power upon earth to forgive sins, (he said unto the sick with palsy,) I say unto thee, Arise, and take up thy couch, and go into thine house. And immediately he rose up before them, took up that whereon he lay, and departed to his own house, glorifying God." (Luke 5:22-26)

We can learn a few things from these scriptures about overcoming the what-ifs. Fueled by faith, the four men's determination to overcome their what-ifs demonstrates their zeal as believers. However, they faced significant obstacles in winning the war over what-ifs:

1. **A crowded, intimidating group of people** — How easy would it have been to look through the door, see the crowd, and say, "Well, Bud, we tried, but as you can see, there are just too many people. We'll have to try another time." No! That thought didn't even cross their minds. Not only was the room crowded, but the scribes and Pharisees were present. The men risked being ridiculed and mocked. But their goal wasn't to please others, only the Lord.

2. **A challenging method** — Scripture doesn't tell us who was the ringleader or if they all simultaneously decided, "Let's go through the roof!" This wasn't the "easy," comfortable part of their mission. It required all four men working together to accomplish something extremely challenging. This strenuous task required solid

and healthy bodies to get the man on the roof and down to Jesus. God picked the perfect men to carry out His plan. The men were physically ready to fulfill their mission.

3. **The hardship of being unified** — All four men had to be willing to pursue the alternative. "Can't get through the front door? Then let's go through the roof!" This wasn't a job for *one* person. It took all of them working together towards a common goal. Have you noticed how unity in our churches, homes, and businesses is under attack? There's power in the unified body of Christ. In the book of Romans, we're taught Christians are to bear one another's burdens. Christians are to be "like-minded one toward another according to Christ Jesus: that ye may with one mind and one mouth glorify God…." (Romans 15:1-6). Is it any wonder the devil works overtime to divide the body of Christ? He knows division is our downfall and weakens our ability and desire to serve the LORD.

To combat adversity, the men exhibited the characteristics of faith-filled, zealous Christians. Four major characteristics stood out:

1. **Compassion** — A Christian with strong faith notices the needs of others. Jude teaches Christians to "Keep themselves in the love of God, looking for the mercy of our Lord Jesus Christ unto eternal life. And of some have compassion, making a difference" (Jude 1:21-22). Notice that the four men didn't judge or condemn their friend. Their goal was to bring him before Jesus, the One who had the power to forgive and heal.

2. **Tenacity** — Tenacity means "the quality of being tenacious, or of holding fast; persistence."[9] These four men were tenacious. Nothing would prevent them from completing their goal. Consider the barriers they surpassed to get their friend to Jesus.

3. **Passion** — Their faith fired them up. They were willing to do whatever it took to get their friend to Jesus. A faith-filled Christian is passionate and will go the distance no matter the cost. The starting point of all accomplishments is desire,

which morphs into passion. On the other hand, feeble desires bring feeble results just as a small amount of fire makes a small amount of heat. Therefore, we need to be passionate about our lives. "Whatever thy hand findeth to do, do it with thy might" (Eccl. 9:10). "Passion is like fire; unless you feed it and stoke it, it will die. Question: On a scale of one to ten, how wholehearted are you about serving the LORD?"[10] "The enemy of passion is indifference. You go through the motions, but other things break your focus. It's not that you said no to God; it's that you haven't said a resounding yes!"[11] "Fan into flame the gift of God, which is in you," (2 Timothy 1:6 NIV). "Neglect not the gift that is in thee" (1 Timothy 4:14).

4. **Desire to glorify God** — Matthew, Mark, and Luke recorded that when the paralytic man rose and walked, those who witnessed the miracle were amazed and glorified God. A zealous, faith-filled Christian will point others to Christ. They're not seeking, nor wanting, others to see

them but the Christ they serve. After the miracle, the four men were never mentioned. All eyes were on their friend and the incredible miracle Jesus performed in his life. There is no record of the friend thanking his four friends. There is no mention of Jesus applauding the four for the extra effort it took to get their friend to Him. Jesus didn't even comment on the method; only their faith caught His attention. A zealous Christian isn't looking for, nor dependent upon, the praise of others. Their goal is to fulfill the work God called them to do. By understanding the work of faith in our lives, we can live zealously. Faith does nothing on its own; faith allows God to do it all. Jesus Christ has won the victory—our victory is in trusting, not in trying. God doesn't seek strong Christians but those who will allow his strength to be made perfect in their weakness.

I read a devotional called the *God-Chip* that helps us understand the importance of placing our faith in God's ability to empower our what-if moments. The author explains that God empowers you to do everything He asks us to do successfully. He transforms us inwardly with a growing desire to serve others, and then He gives us abilities to use in service to others. The Holy Spirit within provides us with the ability to tune into God—to hear Him, to listen to HIM, and to talk with Him. So, please hear this: God didn't create you to fail; He made you to succeed once the Holy Spirit energizes your abilities and empowers your efforts.

Perhaps you noticed the small stickers on many computers that said, 'Powered by [this brand of chip].' In a sense, you have the 'God-chip' powering your life as a follower of Christ. You are empowered by the one and only holy God, who has placed His Holy Spirit within you. God energizes you to live like Jesus. In faith, believe God enables you to succeed. Tell God your fears and ask Him to replace your fears with faith.[12]

Serving the Lord isn't always easy. But He invites you to come to Him during every time of struggle, disappointment, and weakness. Jesus promises to refresh your heart and reenergize your service. "Be steadfast, immovable, always abounding in the work for the Lord; your labor is not in vain" (1 Corinthians 15:58). A zealous Christian will keep the faith and overcome the what-ifs. Your burning faith and love for God and others will ignite the fires of compassion and brightly showcase God's message. Because of your warmth and caring heart, many will be drawn to Jesus. So, my question for you today is: How's your spiritual temperature? Are you fired up? Do you consider others first, and how you can use your talents for the kingdom? The hymn below may serve as an inspiration to put others first and channel our energies toward winning them for Jesus Christ.

Others

Lord, help me live from day to day
In such a self-forgetful way
That even when I kneel to pray
My prayer shall be for – Others.
Help me in all the work I do
To ever be sincere and true
And know that all I do is for You
Must needs be done for – Others.
And when my work on earth is done
And my new work in heaven's begun
May I forget the crown I've won
While thinking still of – Others.
Others, Lord, yes, others,
Let this my motto be; Help me to live for others
That I may live like Thee.

—Charles Meigs (written between 1890 and 1902)[13]

Empowerment through Living Fully Charged Battle Plan:

Reflecting on the phrase "Empowered to Live Fully Charged," I invite you to consider what it truly means to feel empowered and how that influences your daily life. Being fully charged suggests vitality, motivation, and a readiness to engage with the world around you. Ask yourself: In which areas of your life do you feel most empowered? Where might you need to recharge or seek additional inspiration?

Take a moment to evaluate your sources of energy—whether they are physical, emotional, or spiritual—and think about how you can cultivate a state of empowerment that enables you to live intentionally and passionately. Consider how you can support yourself and others in maintaining this charged energy.

Now, I challenge you to identify at least one step you can take today to empower yourself—be it setting a new goal, practicing self-care, or reaching out for support—and commit to maintaining this empowered state regularly. The question I leave with you is: How will you choose to live fully charged today and in the days to come?

Chapter 3
Empowered in the Plot Twist

"God doesn't want something from you.
He wants something for you."
—Unknown Author

I love a good plot twist when watching TV or movies. As a writer, my first reaction is to congratulate the author on their excellent writing skills. Writers face the challenge of engaging viewers/readers through suspense. Plot twists can be fun in entertainment, but unexpected real-life changes can cause panic and despair. Although I've encountered countless what-if moments throughout my seventy-plus years, 2020 was filled with unimaginable plot twists. Little did I realize, along with the rest of the world, what lay ahead when the clock struck twelve.

The first three weeks in January 2020, I was out of town helping my niece care for her mom, who was under hospice care. A few days after she passed, we received startling news about another family member whose path took an unexpected twist. Shortly thereafter, news of a contagious virus quickly spread throughout not only our nation but the world, and we found ourselves sheltering in place.

As the ministry team and I began planning for the 2020 events, we didn't realize that God had His own agenda. Due to the pandemic, our monthly Bible studies were impacted, leading to schedule adjustments and unplanned cancellations. However, we worked through the confusion and were enjoying a prosperous year of ministry.

I was unaware another plot twist was on the horizon as I watched the news about a carrier in the waters close to the venue where I hold my annual ladies' retreat. On September 8, 2019, the Golden Ray (a 200-meter-long car carrier) overturned in the St. Simons Sound near the Port of Brunswick, Georgia. The gigantic carrier was declared a total loss and scheduled to be removed as scrap.

I signed the contract for our retreat with Epworth by the Sea in Saint Simons Island, Georgia, in February and began the planning process. After checking for updates throughout the year and receiving assurance of no changes, the phone call I received on August 19, 2020, left me speechless and in tears. With a broken heart, the Epworth event coordinator shared that the hard decision had been made to cancel all their groups for the remainder of 2020. The company responsible for dismantling the Golden Ray needed to rent Epworth's facilities starting in September, with an undetermined end date.

For the first time in fifteen years, our annual ladies' retreat would not take place! Devastated doesn't begin to describe our emotions. Usually, early November would be a flurry of activity as we made final preparations for the ladies' arrival. On November 14, 2020, the day we would have been at Epworth, I cried as I mourned the absence of our event. As I watched the newscast in August 2019 revolving around the Golden Ray, I was clueless that their accident would have a direct impact on our annual retreat. Whereas I didn't know, God did! Proverbs 16:9 said, "A man's heart plans his way, But the Lord directs his steps."

Reflecting on the unexpected plot twist threatened to plunge me into a deep depression. However, after much prayer, self-reflection, and leaning into the Lord,

I am happy to announce that the enemy didn't win in *my* what-if moment.

Thankfully, even though one door closed, God opened other doors, which included an alternate retreat in January the following year.

What lessons can we learn from the what-ifs?

Below is a list of observations I journaled throughout 2020 after combating one plot twist after another. My prayer is that the lessons I learned will lift others past the "but it's always been this way" mentality. I pray we will strengthen our flexibility as we're confronted with spontaneous detours or roadblocks.

- **God is in control** — A familiar phrase repeated frequently, but has it lost its meaning? Throughout Scripture, we read of God's power and how He is ruler over all things. Knowing this should comfort our minds when the plot twists. We may not know what the future holds, but we know God's authority is sovereign over every detail in our lives—even the uncalculated change of events.

- **God is all-knowing** — God is our ultimate resource and should be the first one consulted for direction and understanding. Proverbs 3:13 said, "Happy is the man *that* findeth wisdom, and the man *that* getteth understanding." In the book of James, we learn that when we lack wisdom, we should ask God. The Living bible paraphrase broadens our understanding of asking God for wisdom.

"If you want to know what God wants you to do, ask him, and he will gladly tell you, for he is always ready to give a bountiful supply of wisdom to all who ask him; he will not resent it. But when you ask him, be sure that you really expect him to tell you, for a doubtful mind will be as unsettled as a wave of the sea that is driven and tossed by the wind; and every decision you then make will be uncertain, as you turn first this way and then that. If you don't ask with faith, don't expect the Lord to give you any solid answer." (James 1:5-8 TLB)

Live in the moment, not the *what-if.* – "Do not boast about tomorrow, for you do not know what a day may bring forth" (Proverbs 27:1). There's a reason God said to take no thought for tomorrow. We can drive ourselves insane when we succumb to worrying about what tomorrow may bring. Worry crushes the spirit. Worry is a waste of energy, yet most of us spend hours out of the day fretting about tomorrow. If we trust God with today, is there a reason not to trust Him with tomorrow? When doubt begins to threaten your faith, remind yourself of these promises: "For I know the thoughts that I think toward you, says the LORD, thoughts of peace and not of evil, to give you a future and a hope" (Jeremiah 29:11).

> "Lord, You have searched me and known me. You know my sitting down and my rising up; You understand my thought afar off. You comprehend my path and my lying down, And are acquainted with all my ways." (Psalms 139:1-3 NKJV)

Embrace the pain and appreciate its value:

As difficult as it is, we need to remember that "pain" is our teacher. Only on challenging paths is faith developed. Only in the strain is faith strengthened. Many of us desire days without hardship or pain. But without them, where would we be? What would we miss? We would miss God's answer to our prayers as we cried out to Him with the faith of a mustard seed. We would miss seeing Him honor unwavering trust in His faithfulness, despite facing unimaginable hardships and uncertainty. We would miss seeing Him work out the "only God could have done that" explanation. We're tempted to avoid suffering, but like Paul, may we embrace suffering so we may "…know him, and the power of his resurrection, and the fellowship of his sufferings" (Philippians 3:10). Another vital value of pain is that it makes us more sensitive to the needs of others, enabling us to comfort others as God comforts us (2 Corinthians 1:4).

Enjoy every season for what it is:

Author John Mason helps us understand that every season has an objective and admonishes us to allow it time to accomplish God's divine plan.

> "Distinctly different things happen during different seasons. God is the God of wintertime. Winter is a season of preparation, revelation, and direction. It's also the time when roots grow. God wants to establish the right foundation in you during this season.

There is no harvest in winter. God is the God of springtime. It's a time of planting, hoeing, and nurturing. In other words, hard work. God wants you to work on your plan. There's no harvest in the springtime. God is the God of summertime. Summer is a time of great growth. Now is the time when activity, interest, and people begin to surround your God-given idea. Despite all the summer activities, there's only a minimal harvest. Then comes autumn. Autumn...this is God's harvest time. During this season, the harvest is reaped in a much greater proportion than the work or activity expended. But most people never make it to the fall. Often, they end up quitting along the way because they don't know what season they're in. Stay in season with God."[14]

Remember, in the end, everything will be okay:

This phrase is near and dear to my heart. One reason is that these were among the last words spoken by my sister, Marie. She was only fourteen months older, but self-appointed as my protector, even in her later days, she comforted and protected me as she weakly whispered, "Everything is going to be okay."

Plot twists exist; avoidance is not an option. Although our future is uncertain, God gives us hope that no one can alter. Do you want to win the war over your *what-ifs*? One last lesson I learned is to "light up and live." I keep this phrase on my desk as a daily reminder, "You cannot kindle a fire in any other heart until it is burning within your own."[15] As I battled my *what-ifs*, one thing that has kept my light lit is feasting on the Word of God. Is your light shining? I encourage you to find your passion. Determine to let your light shine so others can witness the light of God's glory in you. There's someone surrounded by darkness, waiting for your light to shine. After hearing from a good friend about a grim medical diagnosis, without thinking, I blurted, "I'm going to write a song." The alarming news was something I'd rather not have heard. I have never written a song, but I knew God put the idea in my heart.

On the hour drive home, God began pouring the words in my spirit. The verses rushed into my mind, prompting me to park so I could write them down. The song titled "If I Had My Rathers" expressed my desire for a different path for my friend. Next time your what-if moment takes a surprising turn, perhaps you can sing this song of encouragement into your spirit. After all, only in His "rathers" can His best be found.

If I Had My Rathers

If I had my rathers, Lord, I'd choose blessings over pain.
And if I had my rathers, Lord, I'd choose sunshine, not rain.
If I had my rathers, Lord, life would be full of heavenly bliss.
One without sorrow and lots of happiness.

But, from my rathers, Lord, Your Spirit must flee, as only in Your rathers, Lord, is truth made free.
So, I'm trusting in YOUR rathers, Lord, over mine.
Knowing in YOUR rathers, Lord, is glory divine.

Satan is a liar, and he bids me to run.
Away from Your fire, where victory is won.
On the easy road, Lord, I'd rather be.
And walk by sight, so ahead I can see.

But, from my rathers, Lord, Your Spirit must flee, as only in Your rathers, Lord, is truth made free.
So, I'm trusting in Your rathers, Lord, over mine.
Knowing in Your rathers, Lord, is glory divine.

I'm clinging to You, Lord, where perfect peace is found.
I'm leaning on You, Lord, where all hope abounds.
And even when sorrow and suffering come my way.
I know by faith You'll guide me all the way.

So, I'm resting in Your rathers, Lord, over mine.
Knowing in Your rathers, Lord, is glory divine.
I'm trusting Your rathers, Lord, over mine.

Because in Your rathers, Lord, everything's going to
be just fine.
So, I'm trusting in Your rathers Lord, over mine.
Because in Your rathers, Lord, everything's going to
be just fine.

—Billie Corley

Empowerment through Plot Twists Battle Plan:

Reflecting on empowerment through the lens of 'Plot Twist,' consider how embracing the power of belief, submission, and flexibility can transform your perspective in unexpected situations. How do you cultivate faith when life's uncertainties arise? Are there moments when surrender has led to growth? In what ways can being more adaptable help, you navigate life's surprises?

Use this reflection to deepen your understanding of choosing to be empowered, especially when facing the unexpected. Consider how trusting God's plan over your own can bring peace and clarity.

As a call to action, identify one area in your life where applying belief, submission, or flexibility could lead to a positive change. Take a step today to embrace that 'plot twist'—and see how it empowers you to grow.

Chapter 4
Empowered Over the Enemy

"For whatsoever is born of God overcometh
the world: and this is the victory that
overcometh the world, *even* our faith. Who
is he that overcometh the world, but he that
believeth that Jesus is the Son of God?"
—1 John 4:4-5 AKJV

Throughout our Christian journey, we'll encounter countless what-if moments that are bigger than us, but they will never be bigger than God—we have the authority to be empowered over the enemy. Webster defines empowered as: having the knowledge, confidence, means, or ability to do things or make decisions for oneself.[16] A Christian's empowerment comes from God and God alone. When I encounter a situation that is "bigger" than me, I must remember *where* my power comes from. Anything I try in my strength is useless. There is empowerment in education, experience, and hard work. However, we must use all God has made available to us through the indwelling of His Holy Spirit. In His book, *Victory, a Winning Game Plan for Life,* Pastor Chuck Swindoll identifies three things that equip the Christian for victory—birth, faith, and truth.

> "In order to enter into the ranks of the victorious, we must be 'born of God.' Jesus called this process being 'born anew' and/or being 'born again.' This [the new birth] occurs when I accept the gift of eternal life made possible by Jesus' death and resurrection...when I, personally, ask the Son of God to become my Savior from sin. Birth must precede everything. With it, I receive Christ's life, power, and cleansing. Then comes faith. I draw upon the power within me. I no longer operate based on human strength, but by faith, I convert to divine power. And the difference in the two is like that between rumbling along in a twenty-five-ton tank and lifting off the runway in a Phantom jet...and this is the victory that has overcome the world—our faith. It is all made possible by the truth... believing the truth; living in the truth; allowing the truth invade, reshape, and cultivate our lives anew."[17]

I relate to Chuck's three concepts for victory—birth, faith, and truth. Before I became a Christian, I lived a powerless life and was easily persuaded by the ways of the world. God got my attention after a weekend of worldly living. As I drove home, it was as if Jesus sat in the car beside me. Sternly but lovingly, He warned that if I continued the path I was on, death and destruction awaited me. I heeded His warning and began attending church again. Approximately six weeks later, on a Sunday afternoon, I kneeled, confessed my sins, and asked Jesus into my heart. I went to the floor as one individual and stood up as a "new creation…old things…passed away…all things have become new" (2 Corinthians 5:17 NKJV). From that point forward, I was empowered by God's Holy Spirit. As I matured, I learned how to surrender control to God so that His power would be manifested in and through me.

Victory is assured when we invite God into our what-if moments. Defeat is the enemy of empowerment, and empowerment is the enemy of defeat. We see an example of releasing God's power over the enemy through Judah's what-if moment. Prayer, patience, and praise empowered them to move toward victory. We overcome the enemy through prayer. There is an excellent example of this in 2nd Chronicles. When people shared the news of the great multitude coming against Judah, fear gripped King Jehoshaphat's heart. Instead of organizing an army, Jehoshaphat arranged a prayer meeting. His battle plan was to seek God's help through prayer and fasting.

> "And Jehoshaphat feared, and set himself to seek the Lord, and proclaimed a fast throughout all Judah. And Judah gathered themselves together, to ask help of the Lord: even out of all the cities of Judah they came to seek the Lord." (2 Chronicles 20:3-4)

Jehoshaphat's prayer, as recorded in 2 Chronicles 20, acknowledged three things:

- God's position— "…art thou the God in heaven" (Vs. 6a).
- God's authority— "…rulest thou not over all the kingdoms of the heathen?" (Vs. 6b).
- God's power— "…so that none is able to withstand thee?" (Vs. 6c).

He concludes his prayer in a spirit of humbleness as he expresses total dependence upon God. "O our

God, wilt thou not judge them? For we have no might against this great company that cometh against us; neither know we what to do: but our eyes are upon thee" (2 Chronicles 20:12).

Prayer is crucial in winning the war over *what-ifs*. Experience has taught me that I avoid a lot of anguish when I choose prayer as my first defense. Abraham Lincoln once said, "I have been driven many times to my knees by the overwhelming conviction that I had nowhere else to go. My wisdom, and that of those about me, seemed insufficient for the day."[18] In her devotional, *Be Still and Know*, Author Millie Stamm esteems Christians who seek God first rather than attempting to fight the enemy in their own power.

> "Throughout the Bible, often the people of God were driven to their knees in prayer when they were powerless to withstand the onslaught of the enemy." While Jehoshaphat was king of Judah, the land was being threatened by a strong aggressor. The natural plan would have been to recruit more men, step up production of ammunition, and improve their military strategy. But the king knew their resources were insufficient. Only God was powerful enough to conquer their

foe. 2 Chronicles 20:3 told us, "Jehoshaphat feared, and set himself to seek the Lord."[19]

Empowered through patience:

To secure victory against formidable odds, we must rely on God's intervention by choosing to wait. Judah's willingness to wait yielded a substantial win. How many times have we "made our request known unto the Lord" and at once begun "helping Him answer our request?"

Empowered through reliance:

God's battle plan is supernatural, not common sense. Through the Levites, God calmed Judah's fears, assuring them, "the battle is not yours but God's" (2 Chronicles 20:15). Notice, when the enemy *came against* Judah, God *came against* the enemy.

The great multitude thought they were attacking Judah, not knowing that Judah would step aside, allowing God to fight their battle. Romans 8:31 says, "*What shall we then say to these things. If God be for us, who can be against us?* As we surrender our *what-ifs* to God, victory is promised every time! Instead of letting God fight our battles, how many of us waste time and energy fighting Him? The most effective weapon against the enemy rests in God's battle plan. If we insist on fighting the battle according to our wisdom and strength, defeat is inevitable.

Empowered by praise:

Never underestimate the power of praise. What sounds did the Ammonites, Moabites, and Edomites expect at the start of the battle? I think "praise and singing" didn't even enter their mind. The enemy certainly didn't expect a worship service. While Judah offered praises to the Lord, the great multitude destroyed one another. Now that's what I call empowerment to the utmost! It is imperative that we take up our shield of faith and offer praises to the King of Kings and Lord of Lords as we go forth into battle. Judah's victory resulted from their steadfastness and praise offered to the LORD before triumph. When the people of Judah began to sing and praise God, He sent an ambush (a surprise attack) against their enemies (2 Chronicles 20:22).

Jentezen Franklin, author of *Believe That You Can*, has this to say about praising God before the battle.

"Many of us think we have to wait for our complete victory to happen before we can open our mouths and hearts in full worship. But I'm telling you that one way to stir up your faith and joy and energy is to begin to worship on the partial. The deal is this: The joy of the LORD is your strength. If you lose your strength, you lose your power to resist the enemy. If you lose the power to resist the enemy, he will have you for lunch. But if you can worship God, even when all you have in front of you are the foundation stones, the joy of the Lord will fill your heart, and you will not find it so difficult to resist the enemy. 'Resist the devil, and he will flee from you' (James 4:7). If you feel that your faith is getting low, help it out by boosting your joy. The enemy wants you to get depressed. Satan wants you to throw in the towel. The devil wants you to fall into depression, worry, and negative thinking. The antidote is simple-it's worship and praise."[20]

Praising God in the midst of partiality gives us the strength to stand firm in the battle. Because Judah chose praise as their weapon, when the "great company" came against Judah, they met the strong and powerful Hand of God!

Notice the adjectives used to describe Judah's praise fest:

- **Utter Humility**—Jehoshaphat "bowed his head to the ground: and all Judah and the inhabitants fell before the LORD, worshipping the LORD." When we bow our heads and kneel, we communicate to God an attitude of surrender and acknowledgment that He is the Supreme Ruler overall.

- **Absolute Abandonment**—The Levites "stood up to praise the LORD GOD of Israel with a loud voice on high."

- **Unreserved Trust**—Jehoshaphat appointed singers to praise "the beauty of holiness, and, as they went to say, 'Praise the Lord; for his mercy endureth for ever.'" We trust God because His mercies and compassion never end. "*It is of* the LORD'S **mercies** that we are not consumed, because his compassions fail not" (Lamentations 3:22).

When God controls our what-if moments, we can expect colossal results.

Placing absolute faith in God reaps astonishing results. Notice what happened when Judah allowed God to fight their battle (2 Chronicles 20:22-30). The enemy turned on each other. Not one enemy escaped. It took three days to gather the wealth and precious jewels from the dead bodies. They assembled in the valley of Beracah (blessing) instead of the valley of Baca (weeping) (Psalm 84:6). They moved from "having no might" to rejoicing over the enemy!

God was glorified in all the kingdoms. God gave Judah rest from its enemies during Jehoshaphat's remaining reign. Wise is the person who entrusts God with their battle.

Emptying ourselves of our plans prepares the way for God to exercise His authority. Empowerment comes when we invite God into our circumstances. What about you? How are you managing your *what-ifs*? Never forget, even though the *what-if* is bigger than us, it's never bigger than God.

Empowerment through the Enemy Battle Plan:

How do you respond to trials and opposition? Do you turn to prayer as your first action? When facing challenges, are you quick to surrender control to God's authority, or do you struggle to let go?

Have you thought about the power of truly praising God? Is your praise sincere, or is it just words spoken without heart? When you look away from the problem and focus on God's character—His attributes and His love—do you find it easier to stay strong?

Let's make a conscious choice today: take a moment to list God's attributes. Proclaim His greatness and declare His victory over the enemy in your life. Remember, your faith and praise are powerful weapons.

Call to Action: Reflect on your response to life's battles. Cultivate a sincere heart of praise and surrender. Stand empowered, not by your strength, but by God's authority.

Begin this practice today and watch how your perspective and spiritual strength grow.

Chapter 5
Empowered in Weariness

"Your weakness is God's strength. You don't have to worry about your limitations. Do what you can and place all your work in the hands of your heavenly Father. He promises to use things for good in the lives of those who you serve."[21]
— Motivational Card, *Promises from God for Today*

What if your what-if moment finds you physically, mentally, and spiritually drained? Should you continue pushing through? Because of a medical condition, I battle chronic fatigue and am keenly aware of how it feels to be exhausted to the bone. One day while battling fatigue, I prayed, "God, if You choose not to remove my fatigue, then please use it for Your glory."

How should we handle overwhelming fatigue when it strikes in the middle of our *what-ifs*? Is it possible to regain our motivation and energy? It is encouraging to know my lack of energy doesn't limit God in my *what-ifs*. In fact, He uses it!

One day, exhaustion plagued me from morning to midday. As my body begged for a nap, the demands of the day forced me to continue working. To be victorious in my what-if moment that day, I chose extra time in Bible study, which strengthened my spirit. After running a few errands, even though it was apparent my body needed rest, I tackled the to-do list and was thrilled with what I accomplished.

In our fast-paced environment, it's possible to ignore the warning signs of fatigue. We may not recognize that *busyness* is sometimes more harmful than good. Overworking causes our emotions to spiral out of control, and even the smallest task is overwhelming. More than the physical and emotional impact, however, is how this affects us spiritually. We're susceptible to becoming disheartened, losing our joy, and being vulnerable to the enemy's attack.

God's Word teaches three types of weariness:

1. **Physical:** In John 4:6, the word "weary" refers to physical exhaustion. In other words, Jesus was tired.

2. Mental: Hebrews 12:3 speaks of becoming fainthearted.

3. Spiritual: Galatians 6:9 refers to spiritless or without enthusiasm.

How do we stay energized so we can excel in our what-if moment?

*   **Rest** — I know you superwomen are thinking. "Rest? What is that? God designed our bodies to alert us when it's time to relax. Notice what Jesus did when He was weary. He sat down! "Now Jacob's well was there. Jesus, therefore, being wearied with his journey, sat thus on the well: and it was about the sixth hour," (John 4:6). Jesus understood the importance of physical rest so He could continue "doing the will of the Father and finish His work" (John 4:34).

*   **Rehydrate** — Doctors suggest drinking enough water helps to combat fatigue. In John 4:14, Jesus speaks of a well of water that will forever satisfy our spiritual thirst. If your what-if moment has left you spiritually dehydrated, why not sit for a

while, open God's Word, and enjoy sipping on the invigorating waters of His grace?

- **Refresh** — Needing to refresh physically, Jesus took a break from His travels and sat by the well while the disciples went to the city to buy food (John 4:30). By the time they returned, Jesus had witnessed the conversion of a precious soul (John 4:34). There is no better way to empower our what-if moments than seeing God work in the life of another. Don't let a lack of energy hinder you. When necessary, follow Jesus' example and "sit awhile."

Notice what happened after Jesus rested: "After two days he (Jesus) departed" (John 4:43). When we're tired and can't take another step, remember, it's not the end of the journey, it's only a rest stop.

A weary mindset threatens *what-ifs*. We struggle to keep the joy of serving the Lord, and we're tempted to quit. Scripture encourages the Christian not to be weary in well-doing, for in due season we shall reap, if we faint not (Galatians 6:9). Winning requires embracing these straightforward truths, overcoming your uncertainties.

Keep your love for God as the primary motive. Jesus commended the church of Ephesus for their perseverance. However, He said, "I have somewhat against thee because thou hast left thy first love." Not because of their love for the Lord, but for service, the church was implied not to have fainted. Christians will subject themselves to defeat if anything supersedes love for the Father. The task will eventually become burdensome, and joy will diminish. Love for God is an energizer and will keep passion alive. Depend upon God's grace. Our abilities and talents are derived from God's grace. I think of it as "God's power at work through me." Keep the faith. It's easy to quit; it takes faith to go through. Chapter eleven in the book of Hebrews uses the phrase "by faith" fifteen times. One definition of "by" is "indicating the means of achieving something."[22] For instance, God performed incredible miracles through the saints in the Old Testament because of their faith in Him. Faith inspires continued effort despite weariness.

Shift your focus. Loss of momentum signals a need to refocus our attention on Jesus, not wallow in self-pity. Fainting in the mind happens when life's hardships press upon us. "To every *thing there is* a season, and a time to every purpose under the heaven" (Ecclesiastes 3:1). Just as there are four different seasons throughout the year, our lives will include times of joy and sorrow. Instead of focusing on the situation, we can encourage ourselves by changing our mindset. Using Andrew Murray's prayer as an example during a time of illness, we can encourage ourselves by proclaiming:

> "In time of trouble, say, First, He brought me here. It is by His will I am in this strait place; in that I will rest. Next, He will keep me here in his love, and give me grace in this trial to behave as his child. Then say, He will make the trial a blessing, teaching me lessons he intends me to learn, and working in me the grace he means to bestow. And last, say, In his good time he can bring me out again. How and when, he knows. Therefore, say, I am here (1) by God's appointment, (2) in His keeping, (3) under His training, (4) for His time."[23]

Spend time reading and studying scripture. Service is not a substitute for Bible study. Sometimes we're busy working for the Lord and not able to saturate our minds with Scripture. Fellowship with the Lord empowers us to overcome *what-ifs*. God uses His Word to guide our steps, enabling us to apply wisdom in determining which activities to engage in and which to avoid. Choose to keep going. Be your best cheerleader. Hebrews told us, "… for the joy that was set before Him, Jesus endured the cross…" (Hebrews 12:2). Focus on your goal, not the process. As you consider the rewards, you'll be encouraged to move forward.

Take a chuckle-break. Proverbs teach that "A merry heart maketh a cheerful countenance: but by sorrow of the heart the spirit is broken" (Proverbs 15:13). The following poem articulates the confessions of a dog-tired woman. Can you relate? Perhaps after you read the poem, take a nap. After waking up, I'm sure you'll conquer your what-if moment.

Confessions of a Dog-tired Woman

"In the middle of the chaos, what do I find?
A lot of trouble, but I'm trying not to whine.
My never-ending to-do list has me shackled,
I'm told laughter helps; hear me cackle!"
"Better manage your time," per the expert's advice.
To which I sarcastically reply, "That would be nice.
But not a spare moment on my calendar can I find …
To manage my pandemonium or even dine."
The wise man said, "You're at your best when you're
at rest."
I respond, "Surely, you're kidding, surely you jest.
So, what's the solution to my never-ending stress?
Can somebody deliver me from this awful mess?"
"Keep calm," they said, "It will all work out."
"Excuse me; you're not helping," I said with a shout.
"My sanity is gone. My motivation is zapped.
Do not disturb, please. I'm taking a nap."
"Is there a moral to this story? What's the gist?"
"One moment, I'm adding your question to my list."

—Billie Corley

Empowerment through Weariness Battle Plan:

Reflecting on the theme of being empowered through weariness, I realize that life's challenges often leave us feeling exhausted and overwhelmed. Yet, just as God empowered Joshua to lead with strength and purpose amidst great resistance, we too can draw upon divine strength when weariness seeks to dominate us.

When I feel tired and tempted to surrender, I ask myself: Am I aligning my efforts with God's methods? Am I keeping my focus on my God-given purpose? Am I meditating on His promise of success? These questions remind me that empowerment isn't the absence of troubles like weariness. It's the dependence on God who can stand in the gap for us and empower us when we're at our weakest.

Chapter 6
Empowered in the Waiting

"Waiting on God requires the willingness to
bear uncertainty, to carry within oneself the
unanswered question, lifting the heart of
God about it whenever it intrudes upon
one's thoughts."[24]
—Elizabeth Elliott

Victory over the *what-ifs* comes from trusting
God's unseen work. I went to the hospital with severe
inner ear problems two weeks before my ministry's
retreat. Because I was unsure if I could attend my
retreat, I had two choices: have faith or worry. I chose,
as David did in the pit, to wait patiently for the Lord
(Psalm 40:1).

When *what-ifs* threatened my peace, I focused on
God's promises. I decided to: Hope in the Lord, "And
now, Lord, what wait I for? my hope is in thee" (Psalm
39:7). Expect God to intervene on my behalf, "My soul,
wait thou only upon God; for my expectation is from
him" (Psalm 62:5). Rely upon God's strength,
"Because of his strength will I wait upon thee: for God

is my defense" (Psalm 59:9). Place my faith in God's Word, "I wait for the LORD, my soul doth wait, and in his word do I hope" (Psalms 130:5).

I decided to learn the valuable lessons my what-if moment presented: The need to wait solely upon God and not on the result (Psalm 62:5). To fix my mind not on *what* I'm waiting but Who I'm waiting for.

I chose to rest in God's wisdom. When our plans change, it's important to remember that God is guiding us with His eye. "I will instruct thee and teach thee in the way which thou shalt go: I will guide thee with mine eye" (Psalm 32:8). God knows the future and is fulfilling His divine plan.

When I was sitting in the hospital, not knowing if I'd be strong enough to teach at one of my annual retreats, I consoled myself with the knowledge that God was in control. His ways are not my ways, nor are His thoughts my thoughts. During those moments in His waiting room, I remembered that God oversees our what-if moments. As the ruler of the universe, our lives are in His hands, and all the loose ends will eventually fit together perfectly as His plan unfolds.

It's crucial to trust in God's timing, as Dr. Charles Stanley warns in his book *Waiting on God* about the consequences of not waiting on the Lord. He explains that sometimes what seems perfect now might be destructive later, and that God's delays are part of His strategy to arrange all details and prepare us for His best.[25] When pressure mounts and everything around us urges us to move, we should listen to God's instructions, staying like David did— resting in Him and trusting He will work on our behalf.

Waiting on God is not only necessary but also rewarding. God is pleased when His children place their confidence in Him alone, and in doing so, our awareness of His presence deepens. Our hope is restored by remembering that He is our defense, as Psalm 5:11 says, "let all those that put their trust in thee rejoice." He is our shield, as Psalm 18:30 describes, and our provider, as Psalm 37:3 illustrates, assuring us that if we trust in Him and do good, we will dwell securely and be fed. He will bring the desires of our hearts to pass, as Psalm 37:5 promises, and He will put a new song in our mouth, making us testimonies for others to trust Him too, as Psalm 40:3 states. Waiting on the Lord is good; Lamentations 3:26 encourages us that it is beneficial to hope and quietly wait for salvation. God rewards those who patiently wait for Him because He is good to them, as Lamentations 3:25 affirms. Trusting in God's timing can be difficult, especially when we feel paused, but applying these principles helps us overcome the fear of what-ifs.

After being released from the hospital, I attended my retreat, and everything turned out well. Despite needing a walker due to inner ear issues, I managed the weekend—God's presence was there, people were blessed, and lives were changed for His glory. Will you choose to trust God in your what-if moment? True empowerment comes when you trust His timing and His plan.

Empowerment through the Waiting Battle Plan:

Reflecting on being empowered in the waiting, consider how embracing your innate power can transform your experience during uncertain times.

Embrace the power of resting in God's timing. Managing unexpected delays or detours throughout the day can be challenging. What actions can you take to help you successfully maneuver the sudden changes in your schedule?

How do you choose to respond when patience is required? What action can you take to strengthen your trust in God's timing and plan? Make a list of practical ways to build your confidence and trust in God's ability to handle your what-ifs. Remember, empowerment in the waiting is about trusting yourself and trusting God—so take desired steps today to deepen that trust and embrace your power.

Chapter 7
Empowered to Expect More

"Triumph resides in those *what-if* moments,
where faith anticipates abundant blessings
beyond our wildest hopes."
—Billie Corley

Are we expecting God to do superabundantly more in our what-if moment? I pray in faith. I pray, knowing God can do more than I can ask. However, I wonder if I always expect God to show up and show out in my situation? There are times I pray so that I can check prayer off my to-do list. I know I have faith, but sometimes, I feel like the father of the demon-possessed son when he asked Jesus for healing, "Lord, I believe; help thou mine unbelief" (Mark 9:24). Reflecting on possibilities in our what-if moment reminds us that God makes anything possible. We should turn to Him first when facing challenges. In his book, *My Utmost for His Highest*, Oswald Chambers stresses the importance of asking God for the impossible. "If it is an impossibility—it is the thing we have to ask. If it is not impossible, it is not a real disturbance, God will do the absolutely impossible."[25]

One of my go-to verses is Ephesians 3:20. I especially appreciate how The Amplified Bible broadens our understanding.

> "Now to Him who is able to [carry out His purpose and] do superabundantly more than all that we dare ask or think [infinitely beyond our greatest prayers, hopes, or dreams], according to His power that is at work within us, to Him be the glory in the church and in Christ Jesus throughout all generations forever and ever. Amen." (Ephesians 3:20 AMP)

Have you experienced God "showing up" when you least expected Him? In the book of Acts, we meet a man, crippled since birth, who depended on daily transport to the temple for alms. Lying there, watching people pass by and hearing the clunk of coins dropping into his container, was all part of his normal routine. He seemed to expect only his daily needs would be met, relying solely on human assistance rather than divine intervention. After asking Peter and John for alms, Peter commanded the lame man, "Look at us!" Slowly, the lame man raised his head, "*expecting* to receive something *of them*" (Acts 3:5).

Not recognizing God had a life-changing solution, the man anticipated a few coins, enough pocket change to meet the daily need, whereas it was God's purpose to change his life. Sensing God's desire to exceed his expectations, Peter excitedly proclaims, "Silver and gold have I none; but such as I have, give I to thee." If not money, what did Peter possess? The healing, resurrected power of Jesus Christ! In the name of Jesus Christ of Nazareth, Peter empowered a poor, mobility-impaired man, enabling him to walk and experience renewed life. "In the name Jesus Christ of Nazareth rise up and walk." And as Peter lifted the man, his undeveloped ankles and feet received strength. Then, leaping up, he stood, walked, and entered with them into the temple, walking, and leaping, and praising God (Acts 3:6-8).

When God exceeds our expectations, we can anticipate significant changes in our lives. From the desolate places where we once felt trapped, new life will emerge. Our transformation will bring glory and honor to God, causing others to be astonished.

When God shows His power in our what-if moment, we'll recognize a supernatural promise that was waiting to be fulfilled. What was the lame man waiting for? A temporary fix. But God's plan was for something much greater: a permanent solution. His message was clear: "Rise up and walk!"

A Platform for the Miracle

On that day, many wondered whether Peter and John had healed the man. But Peter made it clear that God's power, not their own, was at work. His goal was to shift the focus from the healed man to the God who healed him, encouraging others to seek the Healer rather than just the healing.

Progress in the Pause

The lame man was over forty years old and had lived through Jesus' earthly ministry. Why the long wait? Possibly because a larger audience was needed. As Peter preached about the healing, over five thousand men were saved (Acts 4:4). Although we don't know why it took forty years, we see that God orchestrated these events for a greater impact.

Superpower Provision

When we approach God's throne, are we expecting supernatural intervention? Do we anticipate His active involvement and provision? What are your expectations in your what-if moment? Jesus promised a richer, fuller life. But often, we settle for mere survival. Like the lame man, are we paralyzed by unbelief or ignorance? Was he aware of Jesus' power to heal? Sometimes I catch myself expecting only the bare minimum. But God reminds me: "Billie, I made you for so much more! Rise up! Wise up! Show up! My power can transform your life — mind, spirit, and body." God can change lives. No one needs to remain immobilized in His sight.

God's Message to the Lame Man and to Us Today

To the lame man through Peter: "You were made for more!" To us: "You were made for more." In your what-if moment, remember that you are in the perfect place for God to demonstrate His power. Keep watching and expecting. Your miracle may be just around the corner. Perhaps your miracle is on God's to-do list today. Are you expecting Him to do "superabundantly more than you dare to think"?

Empowerment through Expecting More Battle Plan:

Embrace the power of your potential. Instead of dwelling on what could go wrong, focus on the possibilities of success. Take a moment to write three empowering affirmations that remind you of your strengths and abilities. Let these affirmations inspire your next steps.

Harness the power of action. Turn your what-if scenarios into concrete goals. Choose one specific step you can take this week that brings you closer to your goal. Please write it down, commit to it, and observe how your mindset shifts from doubt to determination.

Embrace the power of setting goals. Close your eyes and imagine your future self—achieving your objectives. Feel the confidence and satisfaction that come with it. Now, create a vision board or a mind map to visualize your path. Let this serve as a daily reminder of your potential.

Every day presents a new opportunity to strive for greater heights and to push beyond your perceived limits. It's important to reflect on whether you truly believe in your own potential and capabilities. Are you consistently taking the necessary steps to achieve more, both personally and professionally? Questions you should ask yourself include: What does 'more' actually look like for me? What goals am I aiming for, and what does success mean in my unique context? What barriers—internal or external—are standing in my way, and how can I effectively work to overcome them? Who are the people in my life that can support, motivate, or challenge me on this journey toward growth?

Today, take some time to identify one specific area where you can push beyond your current limits and comfort zone. Commit to taking a concrete, actionable step toward expecting more from yourself and your life. Remember, growth is a continuous process, and every small step counts. Embrace the challenges, celebrate your progress, and keep moving forward with purpose and determination. Your potential is vast—believe in it, nurture it, and let each day be a stepping stone toward becoming the best version of yourself.

Chapter 8
Empowered in the Overload

"When you face a mountain in your life, you have a choice, be overwhelmed or be energized because you know the Savior will reveal Himself in a profound way to you."[26]
— Charles Stanley

When we're under physical and emotional distress, we're at risk of caving under the load of our what-if moment. While frantically working to check items off the to-do list and maintaining inner peace, it's imperative to stop and readjust so we can unload the overload God's way. Otherwise, we'll sink even deeper into the pile of stress. If an electrical circuit is overloaded, what happens? It's in danger of shutting down or catching fire and won't continue to operate as designed. The same principle applies when our what-if moments are in "overload."

Our minds become overloaded when we carry multiple burdens, such as unresolved emotions like anger, frustration, envy, and sorrow, which fester and grow inside us. Additionally, endless tasks and responsibilities contribute to mental overload, making it difficult to find peace and clarity.

One day, as I stood at a local store's Customer Service Desk, a woman rushed up to the counter, showed her food item and receipt, and offered a quick explanation. The Customer Service Representative placed the item in a bag, handed it to the woman, and she left. Turning to the other CSR who was helping me, he asked, "How can a person forget the one item they came in to purchase?" Although the question wasn't directed at me, I dipped into their conversation, "I know exactly what happened. She needed one item to finish preparing for tonight's event. So, she dashed to the store, grabbed what she needed, ran to the register, paid for it, got the receipt, and dashed off, without the one thing she came for. All the while, her focus remained on the unfinished tasks until the guests arrived. It's called mind-overload." The lady helping me clearly understood. "You are absolutely right," she said. Seeing the confused look on the young man's face, I explained matter-of-factly, "You are a male, and it's difficult for you to understand."

Women often have busy minds. If we're not planning multiple things at once, we think something is wrong. Managing the overload means finding and maintaining a balanced life, which begins in the mind. In his book, *The Battle for the Mind*, Tim LaHaye stresses the importance of mind management. "The mind is to the emotions what food is to the body. For that reason, what the mind feeds upon becomes the most influential force in your life."[27]

When the mind is overloaded, we're at risk of the following:

- Mental collapse: The enemy's goal is to crush the Christian (Luke 22:62).
- Mental burnout: We become exhausted, disheartened, or overwhelmed (1 Kings 19:4).
- Mental stress: Thoughts consumed by unease, worry, or dread (Psalms 143:3-4).
- Mental overload: Overloaded minds experience stress (Luke 10:40).

How do we manage our minds God's way and prevent overload? The first step is guarding the mind.

We can never underestimate the power of our thoughts. Proverbs 23:7 reminds us, "As a man thinketh, so is he." In other words, we become, or eventually live out, what resides in our minds. Have you noticed the battle within your mind? Does it appear that two forces are pulling you in different directions? Years ago, there was a commercial that used images representing good and evil. Both tempted the person into choosing their way of thinking. The individual understandably felt troubled, struggling to make the correct selection. In Romans Chapter Seven, Paul described facing the same dilemma. His new life told him to do right, but the old nature that was still inside of him still wanted to sin. He felt terrible! As his spirit cries out, "Who can deliver me from this great conflict?" He was comforted knowing Jesus Christ won the victory (Romans 7:18-25). This is a lifelong battle. However, as we reflect on our thoughts, it becomes easier to manage them.

The second step is applying the remove and replace principle. Remove thoughts that weaken the mind. It's imperative to remember the battle over the mind is won in the spirit, not the flesh. Only those granted authority are empowered to bring something into captivity.

God has sanctioned that Christians are to exercise authority over the mind.

> "For though we walk in the flesh, we do not war after the flesh: (For the weapons of our warfare are not carnal, but mighty through God to the pulling down of strong holds;) Casting down imaginations, and every high thing that exalteth itself against the knowledge of God and bringing into captivity every thought to the obedience of Christ." (2 Corinthians 10:3-5)

Replace with spirit-building thoughts. An empty mind is subject to attack. Have you ever watched a food commercial on television and felt ravished? That's the power of suggestion. If we're not careful, whatever grabs our attention captures us. Repeating, "I must stop drinking, smoking, etc.," doesn't work because it keeps us thinking about what we don't want to think about. When we replace the thought with something positive, evil loses its grip. Only by reprogramming our minds can we keep them centered on thoughts that edify our spirit and build our faith.

The third step is to empower the mind through our attitude. When the pressure of life overwhelms us, and we feel as if we're about to sink; we can gain altitude through our attitude. A valuable lesson can be learned from Mrs. Reimer, a double amputee. Because of complications from diabetes, Mrs. Reimer had both of her legs amputated, yet she still maintained a joyous attitude toward life. She had to learn to walk again. After her nurse put on the prosthesis, she took a few faltering steps with the aid of her walker. Then, she returned to her bed, sat and beamed, "Imagine, me at ninety learning to walk again. Now that's something!"[28] Mrs. Reimer is an excellent example of how our thoughts help elevate us above our circumstances. Right thinking won't change our situation, but it will influence our ability to lighten the load in our minds.

The fourth step is maintaining peace. In her devotional, Millie Stamm explains staying still in God's presence is necessary but can be difficult because of the noise of the world. "The harder we try, the more difficult it becomes … Yet times of quiet are necessary for our spiritual well-being. Dr. Gilbert Little, a Christian psychiatrist, was asked for a simple rule for mental health. He answered, 'Be still, and know that I am God' (Psalm 46:10)."[29]

One way we can calm our minds is with Philippians 4:8 thinking. As we apply the teachings of this scripture, the result is peace. "Practice what you have learned and received and heard and seen in me, and model your way of living on it, and the God of peace (of untroubled, undisturbed well-being) will be with you (Philippians 4:9 AMPC)."

How did Hannah prevent overload and empower her what-if moment? Hannah was one of Elkanah's two wives. Peninnah, his other wife, had children—it's unclear how many, but Scripture tells us, "sons and daughters." Hannah was barren because the LORD had closed her womb. Elkanah loved Hannah and tried to comfort her by giving her double portions. Her adversary, through Peninnah, stirred her emotions, causing mental distress. The adversary harassed Hannah year after year and wouldn't stop until he pushed her over the edge. Notice the signs of Hannah's overload (1 Samuel 1:7). She wept. She did not eat. She was mentally burdened, her mind restless. Hannah's actions during her what-if moment showed her unloading burdens the way God intended. She trusted the Lord with her overload.

> "In her deep anguish Hannah prayed to the LORD, weeping bitterly. And she made a vow, saying, "LORD Almighty, if you will only look on your servant's misery and remember me, and not forget your servant but give her a son, then I will give him to the LORD for all the days of his life, and no razor will ever be used on his head." (1 Samuel 1:10-12 NIV)

When the weight of her what-if moment was unbearable, Hannah released her burden through prayer. Notice: Hannah took her burden to the Lord rather than turning to her husband or priest for help. Hannah continued praying until she received a word from the Lord.

> "As she kept on praying to the Lord, Eli observed her mouth. Hannah was praying in her heart, and her lips were moving but her voice was not heard. Eli thought she was drunk and said to her, "How long are you going to stay drunk? Put away your wine. "Not so, my lord," Hannah replied, "I am a woman who is deeply troubled. I have not been drinking wine or beer; I was pouring out

my soul to the Lord. Do not take your servant for a wicked woman; I have been praying here out of my great anguish and grief." Eli answered, "Go in peace, and may the God of Israel grant you what you have asked of him." (1 Samuel 1:12-17 NIV)

Hannah's prayer wasn't a half-hearted, bullet prayer; she poured out her soul to God as she lingered in His presence and listened for His answer.

Using Hannah's example, we can expect to manage our overload God's way, and in doing so, the following will happen:

- Faith will be restored. –1 Samuel 1:18
- Peace will return. –1 Samuel 1:18
- Joy will replace sorrow. –1 Samuel 1:18
- Praise will replace bitterness. –1 Samuel 1:19
- God's blessings will fill the barren areas of our lives. –1 Samuel 1:19-20
- We will accept God's perfect timing. –1 Samuel 1:20
- God will receive all the glory. –1 Samuel 1:20, 26-28

- We will gladly return to the Lord, His blessings.
  –1 Samuel 1:28
- Our hearts will once again overflow with thankfulness and praise. – Samuel 2:1-2

Hannah's adversary relentlessly provoked her, "year after year," as she went up to the house of the Lord with her husband and his other wife. Hannah reached a point where she had had enough and decided to cast her burden onto the Lord. God rewarded Hannah for inviting Him into her situation by granting her a son, Samuel, who became a prophet, priest, and judge over Israel. What about you? How do you handle your overload? Do you cast it on the Lord, or do you drag it around aimlessly as you try to manage the burden alone? Praise the Lord, He's ready and able to take the load when we cast our cares upon Him.

Empowered through the Overload Battle Plan:

Are you feeling overwhelmed by the busyness of life? Have you taken a moment to listen to your thoughts lately? What are you experiencing mentally right now? Is your mind at peace, or is it weighed down by stress? Consider how awareness can empower you. What steps can you take to become more in tune with your inner state?

Have you tried journaling your thoughts and feelings? How might tracking what you allow into your mind help lighten your emotional load? Are you engaging in daily reflection or memorization of meaningful words? How could meditating on inspiring scriptures or affirmations influence your sense of peace and purpose?

What practical actions can you implement today to embrace these powerful tools and find balance amid the overload?

Remember, empowerment begins with awareness and proactive habits. What is one step you can take now to nurture your mind and spirit?

Chapter 9
Empowered in the Unexpected

"Being in God's will gives you confidence,
but it won't always make you comfortable.
Following a plan you didn't devise, to a
destination you see in your mind but can't
explain, is called 'walking by faith.' God
decides the plan, moves you from point A to
point B, and says, 'Trust Me; I've got it all
worked out.'"[30]
— *The Word for You Today*

Living empowered means God has instilled in us everything needed to be overcomers, even when life seems to go in an unimaginable direction. How do we cope when our what-if moments are filled with surprising scenarios? Is it possible to find strength and determination even when bitterness threatens our souls? Through an Old Testament saint named Naomi, we will learn that empowerment in the unexpected is achievable and rewarding.

When I first saw the title, Change Your Words, Change Your Life, I thought it was incorrect because one cannot change one's life by merely speaking words. However, after persevering through an almost unbearable test to identify inner ear issues, I have a better understanding of the influence behind "change your words, change your life."

My ear, nose, and throat doctor ordered an inner ear exam known as a balance test. Unless you've had one, there's no way to comprehend how overwhelming this test is to patients. The extensive procedure involves flushing water in the ears four times, twice in each ear. The rushing of water causes extreme dizziness and nausea. The sensation is much like diving into a pool. After flushing my ears the first time, I wondered if I could endure the remainder of the test. The otologist advised that it was my decision whether to continue. The conclusion would be incomplete; nevertheless, I had a choice. She further explained that feeling dizzy was a positive reaction and suggested that when the dizziness began to repeat, "Dizzy is good" to help me tolerate the test. During the duration of the test, I enthusiastically declared, "Dizzy is good! Dizzy is good!" Thankfully, I completed the test. All because I opted to engage in positive self-talk. It didn't change the situation, but it changed my ability to withstand the discomfort.

When the *what-ifs* don't go our way, God has plans of His own—better plans. Remember, God is not limited and works within an environment without time or space. He knows the past, present, and future and isn't confined to the immediate crises of the hour but looks beyond our days and sees our tomorrows. His wisdom and authority over all creation guide us toward His expected end (Jeremiah 29:11). All He asks of the Christian is to surrender to His leadership over our lives.

When life doesn't turn out as we planned, we can rejoice in the possibility that God is redirecting our path to greater blessings. We can see this principle through the life of Cliff Barrows, the renowned musician known for playing alongside Billy Graham, a well-known evangelist.

> "Years ago, in 1945, prior to meeting Billy Graham, Cliff Barrows and his fiancée scraped together enough funds for a simple wedding and two train tickets to a city with a resort hotel. On arrival, however, they found that the hotel had shut down. Stranded in an

unfamiliar city with little money, they thumbed a ride. A sympathetic driver took them to a grocery store owned by a woman he knew. The newlyweds spent their first night in the room above the store. The next day, when the lady overheard Cliff playing Christian songs on his trombone, she arranged for them to spend the rest of their honeymoon at a friend's house. Several days later, the host invited them to attend a youth rally where a young evangelist was speaking. The song leader that night was sick, and Cliff was asked to take charge of the music. The young evangelist, of course, was Billy Graham. The two became partners from then on."[31]

Various personalities or previous experiences influence how we respond to life's surprises. For example, a person's behavior depends on personality, family background, physical or mental health, level of spiritual maturity, and other factors. Here are a few examples of how different people react when life throws a curveball: The planner is devastated because this wasn't on the list. A prayer warrior immediately prays, seeking God's guidance and comfort. A controller tries to manipulate the situation to fit their own understanding. A weak-minded person quickly gives up. A patient person waits on the Lord. A strong-willed person decides to push through. A dependent person expects someone else to step in and take over. A leader forms a committee to develop an action plan. The gossiper will tell everyone about their troubles. A private person suffers in silence. An immature person sulks and pouts. Can you relate to any of these examples when facing unpredictable situations?

Scripture teaches how a Christian should react in times of the unexpected. Here are a few examples:

- Trust God – "Trust in the LORD with all thine heart and lean not unto thine own understanding. In all thy ways acknowledge him, and he shall direct thy paths" (Proverbs 3:5-6).
- Live joyfully – "Be joyful in hope, patient in affliction, faithful in prayer" (Romans 12:12 NIV).
- Living fearlessly – "Do not be afraid of what you are about to suffer" (Revelation 2:10a NIV).
- Surrender to God's will – "Father, if thou be willing, remove this cup from me: nevertheless, not my will, but thine, be done" (Luke 22:42).

An Old Testament saint named Naomi is an example of one's reaction after unexpected losses. Because of a famine in Bethlehem-Judah, her husband, Elimelech, moved Naomi and their two sons to the country of Moab. After his death, Naomi and her sons stayed in Moab, where they both took wives from the women of Moab. One's given name: Orpah; the other's: Ruth. They dwelt there about ten years, and the two sons, Mahlon and Chilion, died (Ruth 1:1-3). In biblical times, prior to support via life insurance, retirement plans, pension, plus investments, the woman, upon her husband's death, depended upon her sons. Since Naomi had neither a husband nor sons, she had no means of support. She heard that the Lord had provided food for His people and decided to return to her homeland.

Caring a great deal for her daughters-in-law, she encouraged them to remain in Moab so they could marry and bear children. Initially, both traveled with her; however, Orpah decided to return. Ruth begged Naomi to allow her to continue the journey with her. As Naomi and Ruth entered the city, the people gathered around asked, "Is this Naomi?" To which she replied:

"Call me not Naomi, call me Mara; for the Almighty hath dealt very bitterly with me. I went out full, and the LORD hath brought me home again empty. Why then call ye me Naomi, seeing the LORD hath testified against me, and the Almighty hath afflicted me?" (Ruth 1:20-21)

In her time of sorrow and grief, Naomi no longer wanted to hear her name, which meant "pleasant," but preferred Mara, which means "bitter."

When Naomi's what-if moment didn't go as planned, initially, she couldn't see beyond her loss.

Perhaps as she and Ruth traveled the road back home, memories of her and Elimelech's trip to Moab flooded her mind. I imagine tears forming as Naomi recollected the happier times. It was a bleak time in the history of Judah. Yet the plentiful resources in Moab offered a more promising future. Still, I can visualize Naomi revisiting the memory of her and Elimelech holding hands and walking side by side, dreaming of a long and prosperous life, which caused grief to prick her heart. Tears probably began to run down her cheeks as she recalled how they had anticipated the boys growing up, marrying wives, and giving them lots of grandchildren. The journey to Bethlehem-Judah had to have been a painful reminder that returning home without them wasn't a part of the plan. A root of bitterness threatened to grow and pollute her soul. Thankfully, this was short-lived, and she didn't succumb to a life filled with anger and resentment.

What empowered Naomi to overcome her heavy spirit? Naomi refused to put on the mask. Naomi's response to the crowd's greeting appeared harsh, but it expressed her heart. At first, Naomi wanted to change her name because her situation had changed. God has the freedom to teach an honest heart when it's not filled with pretense (Ruth 1:20-21). Naomi accepted acts of kindness from others. Ruth was young and able-bodied, with the strength to endure the hard labor required to glean the fields for food. She asked Naomi if she could gather food, to which Naomi replied, "Go, my daughter" (Ruth 2:2). Had bitterness dominated Naomi's spirit, her response would have been much sharper. She could've said something like, "Why bother? You're a stranger. No one will allow you to enter their field. We might as well plan to die as our husbands have." A bitter spirit shuts another out. A wounded spirit on the path to healing will welcome others in. Thankfully, Naomi was well on her way to emotional healing and headed towards God's plan for her life. Naomi received God's loving kindness.

After gleaning the fields, Ruth returned with grain and leftovers from her lunch. When Naomi inquired about whose field she had gleaned, Ruth couldn't talk fast enough as she described the events of her day. When Naomi heard the field belonged to a man named Boaz, she gave God total praise rather than crediting her good fortune to chance (Ruth 2:20).

Naomi sought the welfare of others. A person whose life is consumed with bitterness is self-centered. Their needs. Their wants. Their pain. Their loss. Someone else's happiness is a painful reminder of their hardship. They are more interested in feeding sorrow than in being a blessing to another. They have no time for anyone else unless the person has something they want. Naomi's unselfishness is evident when she became a matchmaker and devised a plan on how to get Boaz and Ruth together (Ruth 3:1-6). Naomi ministered to others in their time of distress. She communicated concern and understanding when she assured Ruth that Boaz would fulfill his intentions (Ruth 3:18).

In the end, Naomi's life glorified and honored the Lord. In Ruth 4:14, we see the same women who greeted Naomi on the day of her arrival giving the Lord praise. They witnessed her transformation from bitterness to blessedness. All because Naomi allowed God's power to strengthen her in her unexpected what-if moment.

Naomi managed her what-if moment with dignity, grace, and endurance. The life she and her husband planned took an unexpected turn. Yet, God empowered her to remain steadfast, and because of that, this inspiring story ends with Naomi holding her grandchild, Obed, who is the father of Jesse, the father of King David. All because Naomi elected God's power over the power of bitterness, releasing her from bondage and a life filled with heavenly bliss.

Is your what-if moment overwhelmed with unanticipated events? Were your plans and dreams for the future interrupted by an unforeseen loss? Have heartache, anger, and bitterness hindered your ability to move forward to a better, brighter future? If you are overwhelmed by the what-ifs, it is my prayer, like Naomi, that you discover God is working all things together for your good, so that you can receive in abundance all He has purposed for you.

You'll find ample power to persevere in your what-if moment once you determine to go where you will receive God's blessings. Embrace the power of generosity. Naomi had few material things to offer Ruth, but she gave that which she had: love, wisdom, guidance, and encouragement, and God used her to guide Ruth's path. What can you give in your season of loss? Someone, somewhere, has a need that only you can meet, even in your unexpected season of loss.

Empowerment through the Unexpected Battle Plan:

"The burden of suffering seems a tombstone
hung about our necks, while in reality it is
only the weight which is necessary to keep
down the diver while he is hunting for
pearls."[32]
—Johann Paul Friedrich Richter

Reflecting on being Empowered in the Unexpected, consider a time when your plans didn't unfold as anticipated. How did you respond to the surprises and uncertainties? Did you lean into your feelings and seek guidance rooted in your faith? Embracing the power of perspective can help us see beyond immediate circumstances and recognize God's purpose in every situation. When faced with the unexpected, how can we adjust our outlook to align with God's Word?

Similarly, think about the power of determination in the face of adversity. Like Naomi, who was in a challenging situation yet chose to listen for God's visitation and followed His lead, how can we develop that same resilience? Are there moments when you've had to decide to move forward despite difficulties?

As you reflect, consider how you can empower yourself today to embrace the unexpected with faith and determination. What steps can you take to trust God's plan more fully? I encourage you to write down your thoughts and commit to trusting God's process, even when it leads you into the unknown.

Chapter 10
Empowered over Impatience

"Why wait? Because without God, I don't
have deliverance… I don't have security… I
don't have hope… I don't have any glory…
I don't have any refuge. I am helpless."[33]
—Charles R. Swindoll

Are you in need of patience? Dig deep because it's in there. God's power, through Jesus Christ, is the indwelling presence of His Spirit. Patience is derived from His resurrection power, enabling you to overcome the *what-ifs*. Colossians 2:8-9 reminds us we're "complete" in Christ. For a Christian, being patient should come naturally, allowing us to endure the trials. However, many of us, like the psalmist David, long to fly away from our troubles. "And I said, Oh that I had wings like a dove! *for then* would I fly away and be at rest" (Psalm 55:6). Throughout scripture, God tells us to cling to Him during difficult times. He consistently instructs us to come close to Him, the One who commands the light to shine out of darkness. Our Lord encourages His people to walk with Him through the stormy waters, allowing Him to be our strength as He reveals great and mighty things we don't yet know. As He shows us the treasures hidden in darkness and opens our minds to the riches of His grace.

Author Charles R. Swindoll shared a great reflection on the theme of patience and endurance:

> "I have read a lot of good stuff about waiting and developing endurance, but I've never read anything better on that subject than J. B. Phillips' paraphrase of James 1:2-4. Please read these words very slowly and thoughtfully. After you have finished, pause and pray. Ask the Lord to give you the strength to wait… to endure the lingering test of patience.
>
> 'When all kinds of trials and temptations crowd into your lives, my brothers, don't resent them as intruders, but welcome them as friends! Realize that they come to test your faith and to produce in you the quality of endurance. But let the process go on until that endurance is fully developed, and you will find you have become men (women) of mature character with the right sort of independence. (James 1:2-4, Phillips).'"[34]

Impatience is not your friend. The spirit of impatience will cause you to miss God's best for your life. Impatience is a sin of unbelief and lack of faith; a poor testimony for the cause of Christ, and an ungodly attitude that must be dealt with. Where does impatience come from? Partly, the source of impatience is the surroundings in which we live. The fast-paced lifestyle is ingrained in us, and patience has been replaced with the expectation of immediate results. Words associated with impatience are annoyance, exasperation, irritation, edginess, restlessness, nervousness, and intolerance.

Impatience is the work of the flesh and the devil. He will do everything he can to hinder spiritual maturity. He wants us to remain dormant, ignorant, and spiritually bankrupt. The last thing he wants is a wise and mature Christian who has learned to "patiently wait upon the Lord." The enemy of our souls knows impatience will weaken our faith, entice unwise choices, and generate discouragement and despair. When we choose *not* to tap into the Spirit of patience, we can expect the fruit of impatience to grow. We will walk aimlessly through the difficulties, and when it ends, we will not have benefited from its purpose. Most likely, if you are a Christian, the Holy Spirit has convicted you that this is an area that needs to be frequently confessed and guarded.

An impatient person is not pleasant to be around. My husband will attest to that statement. I hesitated to include this chapter in my book because "I want to hurry and finish." I battled "rushing" to get to the end, and the fruit of impatience has overflowed, causing my husband to want to sit quietly in the recliner.

Impatient people, especially if they are Christians, are a poor witness for the cause of Christ. Do we read in Scripture anywhere that Jesus was impatient? I think not. And He is our example; we are commanded to be Christlike in all our ways. "Not that I have now attained [this ideal], or have already been made perfect, but I press on to lay hold of (grasp) *and* make my own, that for which Christ Jesus (the Messiah) has laid hold of me *and* made me His own" (Philippians 3:12 AMP).

What are the physical signs of impatient people? They sigh frequently. They roll their eyes and may tap their fingers on a hard surface or place their hands on their hips. Then there is "that look." They don't say anything with their mouths but communicate as loudly as possible through body language. When walking with someone moving at a slower pace, an impatient person might grab their hand and pull them along. They often glance at their watch. If they are behind another car at a traffic light, the moment the light turns green, they repeatedly "honk the horn." Has this ever happened to you? My first reaction is to get out of my car, slowly walk back to the driver, and with a sweet, slow southern drawl, ask, "You honked? Did you need to speak to me?" Just to be clear, this isn't a display of the Holy Spirit at work but rather a manifestation of the flesh when patience isn't allowed to prevail.

An impatient person will interrupt while someone else is talking. A customer service representative at the Post Office where I used to live was an "over-the-top" impatient person. As soon as I stepped up to the counter, he'd speed through the transaction while blurting out the mandated questions. His demeanor, like a neon sign, shouts "impatient." At the same time, I frantically fumbled through my purse for my wallet. I didn't like when he "waited on me." Although one could never use the word "wait" to describe his customer service skills. From my viewpoint, he needed more training on how to "wait well." If I had questions, I hesitated to ask because his actions communicated, "he didn't have the time." In contrast, there was another gentleman who was the opposite; he patiently served me. I didn't feel rushed; rather, I felt relaxed.

His demeanor demonstrated patience, even in dealing with my issues.

Patience is often associated with words like long-suffering, perseverance, calm, endurance, staying power, serenity, tolerance, being uncomplaining, persistence, fortitude, strength, courage, resilience, and flexibility. Reflect on whether someone might describe you using any of these words. Impatience, however, brings about problems, one of which is the message it sends to God. When we choose impatience over patience, we communicate that we think God is in our way, that we want what we want immediately, and that our plan is better than His. We may feel we've waited long enough, prefer walking by sight, or believe that God has forgotten us. Sometimes, we trust our own judgment more than His, thinking we've prayed enough or expect Him to bring answers quickly.

Essentially, impatience signifies a lack of trusting in God's timing and plans.

WOW! Did you find it difficult to read the above words? I did. We often underestimate the significance of the message we convey to our Lord when we choose not to wait on Him. Not to honor Him with the virtue of patience.

Another danger is failure to display Christ-like behavior (Matt. 18:23-35).

The following parable is about forgiveness; however, it also involves patience towards others:

A man owed an enormous debt, which he could not pay. The king threatened to sell him, his wife, and children and all he had to pay off the debt. The servant begged the king to "have patience with him and he would pay his entire debt." The king, moved with compassion, granted him his request. An individual still owed debt to the man the king pardoned. However, when that person begged for *patience*, he failed to extend it. When the king heard what he had done, he revoked the decision and "delivered him to the tormentors, till he should pay all that was due him" (Matthew 18:34).

God's word clearly teaches we reap what we sow. If we extend patience *to* others, we will reap patience *from* others. Therefore, we're not only a positive testimony for the cause of Christ; we benefit when we sow the seeds of patience.

An inpatient person faces the risk of missing God's best, similar to Esau, who lost his divine inheritance (Gen 25:30-34). We might also interfere with God's plans like Abraham and Sarah did (Genesis 16:1-16) or squander our inheritance prematurely (Luke 15:12-14). Additionally, there's the danger of not finishing our course (Galatians 6:9; 2 Timothy 4:7). Another significant risk is acquiring debt, influenced by a culture of "instant gratification" that promotes a "buy now, pay later" mindset. Many are tempted to borrow money to hasten the lifestyle they desire, often aiming to own residences soon after marriage, without the patience to save and wait. It's important to be cautious of get-rich-quick schemes and living on credit, because God's timing and ways are best for prosperous living.

Lastly, impatience grieves the heart of God (Ephesians 4:30; Galatians 5:22). Yielding to impatience is a sin, as it dishonors the Holy Spirit and hinders spiritual growth. However, when we surrender to God's Spirit, we are empowered to overcome these temptations. Patience and trust in God's plan are essential virtues in our spiritual journey.

The Amplified Bible defines long-suffering as not only "the ability to wait, but how we act while waiting" (Gal 5:22 AMP). James teaches that we should not just be "hearers of the word, but doers also."

Below are ways we can demonstrate patience before the Lord as we honor this valuable attribute that He has graced us with.

- We need to wait steadfastly. (Psalms 25:5)
- We need to wait courageously. (Psalms 27:14)
- We are to wait quietly. (Psalms 37:7-9; Lam 3:26)
- We are to wait patiently. (Psalm 37:7, Psalms 40:1)
- We need to wait prayerfully. (Psalms 40:1b)
- We need to wait purposefully. (Psalms 59:9)
- We need to wait expectantly. (Psalms 39:7; Lam 3:25)
- We need to wait only on God. (Psalms 62:5-6)

- We need to wait on God to fulfill His promises. (Psalms 130:5; Heb 6:15)
- We need to wait actively. (Psalm 130:5-8)
- We need to wait trustingly. (Romans 8:18-25)
- We need to wait wisely. (2 Tim 4:5)
- We need to wait joyfully. (James 5:11)

These words can be hard to hear; I feel the spirit of impatience in myself more often than I'd like. If you feel the same, remember, you are empowered! God has equipped us to be overcomers—even when impatience seems to have won. Or maybe you're a patient person, and these truths don't seem to apply to you. But God may bring someone your way who needs to hear this. As they share their struggles, you can tell them, "I just read something I believe will help."

I encourage you to look up the Scripture references. Spend time meditating on one of the fourteen concepts for the next two weeks. Let the Holy Spirit speak to you and teach you how He has empowered you to "wait patiently" on Him.

When I reflect on patience, I often think of one of my favorite writers and speakers. Author Ann Kiemel

Anderson, a best-selling author and inspirational speaker, encouraged me to become a speaker and teacher of God's Word through her life's work and teachings. Her words and examples inspired me to pursue a similar path, emphasizing the importance of perseverance and patience in life's long journey. Ann believed that the long haul separates the truly committed from those less willing to pay the price, reminding us that in waiting, God is working out His plan and that only we can decide if the wait is worth it.

Empowerment through Impatience Battle Plan:

Accept the strength found in patience. Think about which areas you find difficult to wait on the Lord. What actions can you take to change your attitude or behavior?

Accept the strength found in enduring hardships. Do you agree with Paul, "glory in your infirmities, that the power of Christ may rest upon you"? (2 Corinthians 12:9). Reflect on how you handle difficult times and what gives you strength during those moments. Which areas could use improvement?

Accept the strength found in perseverance. You are more resilient than you realize. Recall some tough seasons you've gone through. What lessons did you learn about yourself? Remember how God empowered you to carry the burden until He brought moments of renewal.

Chapter 11
Empowered Through Joy

"Your mind is like the womb of your spirit;
it nurtures each seed you sow until the time
of delivery. If you don't want what a seed
will ultimately produce, you must stop
sowing it and feeding it."[35]
—Jentezen Franklin

At the arrival of trouble, most likely, our first thought isn't "Oh joy!" Rather, our minds begin swirling out of control as the what-ifs threaten with thoughts of panic and despair. Is it possible to experience an attitude of joy during times of pain and suffering? For some people, the answer is, "Absolutely!" For others, their reply is in the form of a question: "Is an attitude of joy during times of hardship even possible?" The fundamental fact to consider is that we have a choice. We can choose to lead our minds toward joy, or we can remain bound by the relentless what-ifs. Many of us don't choose a complicated or challenging life; sometimes it chooses us. But we can definitely choose our response to it. Experiencing hardship and pain in life is inevitable, but choosing to be miserable is optional.

Author Lloyd Ogilvie tells of a Christian friend who was physically and emotionally depleted because of extreme pressures.

> A depressed mood engulfed him. When Ogilvie asked him how he was doing, he said grimly, "Well, joy's certainly not an option!" Ogilvie replied, "You're right! Joy is no option. It's your responsibility. Shocked, the friend retorts, "You talk about joy as if it were a duty." Ogilvie responded, "Right again!" He explained that we have a duty to God, ourselves and others to overcome our moods and to battle through to joy."[36]

How would you respond? I've learned over the years that counting it all joy in the *what-ifs* is not only possible but becomes easier as our faith grows. God granted us the ability to exercise authority over our minds so that we can interject happy thoughts, even during the severest of trials. The word "count," as used in James 1:2, is a verb. Therefore, when we face troubles of any kind, we should immediately exercise authority over our thoughts, i.e., command our minds to be cheerful and happy. Happy because of the hardship? No, glad because God has a purpose in the hardship. Our "count it all joy" moments may not always be pleasant, as the testing of our faith seldom is, but we can calm our minds,' knowing God is maturing our faith. An attitude of calm delight strengthens our minds as we contemplate that God is doing a greater work within us than that which is going on around us.

Author Joe Stowell points out an intriguing truth with the reminder that James doesn't tell us to *feel* joy.

> "If we are to respond constructively, we must understand that James 1:2 does not tell us to *feel* joy. For that we can be thankful. It's impossible for us to manipulate our emotions. Emotions are a result of circumstances, body chemistry, how we have slept, what we have dreamed, or even what we may have eaten the night before. When I'm not feeling right about things, I don't have a joy button that I can press and suddenly feel wonderful. For the most part, emotions come and go and are often dictated by the circumstances of life. And although we are usually able to keep our emotions in check, it's impossible to change them

dramatically. Emotions are the baggage that comes with our trouble."[37]

If we were a robot without emotion, heeding God's instructions to "count it all joy" would come about easily. God designed emotions, not to hinder us, but as a vehicle to living the abundant life. Emotions are a powerful influence and can thrust us forward or, if not managed correctly, plunge us into the depths of despair.

As mentioned, choosing joy requires exercising authority over our thoughts and leading our mind away from doubt, discouragement, despair, and defeat onto an attitude of cheerfulness.

The Living Bible paraphrases James 1:2-4 as:

> Dear brothers, is your life full of difficulties and temptations? Then be happy, for when the way is rough, your patience has a chance to grow. So let it grow, and don't try to squirm out of your problems. For when your patience is finally in full bloom, then you will be ready for anything, strong in character, full and complete. (James 1:2-4 TLB)

How would you paraphrase James 1:2-4? Perhaps one interpretation would read like this: As soon as I sense myself covered up by trouble, I will take authority over my thoughts and select gladness, rather than fretting, knowing God has allowed this trial to test my faith and build up within me His Holy Nature.

Counting it all joy when we fall into various temptations enables us to embrace the adversity so that we reap the benefit of its purpose. Dr. Charles Stanley stresses the importance of embracing adversity.

> "Far more important than the source of adversity is the response to adversity. Why? Because adversity, regardless of the source, is God's most effective tool for deepening your faith and commitment to Him. The areas in which you are experiencing the most adversity are the areas in which God is at work. When someone says, 'God is not doing anything in my life,' my response is always, 'So then, you don't have any problems?' Why? Because the best way to identify God's involvement in your life is to consider your response to adversity. God uses adversity, regardless of the source. But the response determines whether God can use it to accomplish His purpose. In fact, adversity can destroy your faith. If you do not respond correctly, adversity can put you into a tailspin from which you may never recover. It all hinges on your response."[38]

Wow! Did you catch that? "If you don't have problems, means God isn't doing anything in your life!" Surely, that is ample motive to "count it all joy!" With the trial comes "the knowing" God is working in your life. And everything God does is good! Because the goodness of God is active in your situation, we can consider the hardships, the pain, the suffering, the trial, the trouble, and the joy!

My spirit overflowed with joy while typing the above paragraph. It is my prayer that you will allow God to empower you with His joy the next time you "fall into various trials." Joy is your cheerleader and will see you through the times of tribulation.

Choosing joy is not only a choice but also managing our emotions and embracing adversity. It's exercising discernment in the face of temptation. It may be said that both trials and temptations are often sides of the same coin. This is to say that both God and Satan may be working in the life of a believer through the same event, one to purify him, the other to pervert him.[39]

As we immediately lead the mind to joy in the face of trials and temptations, the confusion clears, enabling us to discern who is at work: God to bring out the best in us or the devil to bring out the worst in us. Remember, even in a perfect environment, the enemy can deceive the mind. Take Eve, for example. She lived in a setting not yet tainted by sin. Her body wasn't infiltrated with evil, yet she succumbed to deception. Notice Satan even used God's Word as trickery: "*Yea hath God said…*" (Genesis 3:1). He attacked the tranquility of her mind by placing seeds of doubt and confusion. Now, pay close attention to what areas of Eve's body were instrumental in influencing her decision.

And when the woman **saw** that the tree was **good for food**, and that it was pleasant to the **eyes**, and a tree to be desired to make **one wise**, she took of the fruit thereof, and did eat (Genesis 3:6, emphasis mine).

Notice the process and that Eve *saw* with her *eyes* (a gateway to the mind), reasoned in her *mind* (thoughts), and *ate* the forbidden fruit (action). She allowed what the serpent said to overrule God's commandments. Therefore, her spirit was penetrated with darkness. Had she immediately taken the thought captive and brought it before God, she would not have been deceived. This is a solemn reminder that even a spirit-filled Christian is susceptible to the enemy's attack. It's imperative to maintain a sober mind—one that is alert and constantly on guard. A good example is the mind of a soldier. Since the enemy could lurk in the shadows, he must constantly be on guard. If he allows himself to be distracted, he's vulnerable to attack.

Two Old Testament giants faced a "giant" of a problem: one, a perceived giant, the other, a literal giant. Let's examine what they saw, what they thought, and their reaction.

First, there's Elijah, a mighty prophet who God miraculously sustained during a drought. One who fearlessly defeated 450 prophets of Baal. Rightly, we could conclude that nothing could disturb his faith in the Almighty. However, after winning a glorious victory, the opponent, in his what-if moment, *one woman* (granted, she was mean) sent him running for his life (1 Kings 17, 18, 19). In contrast, in King David's what-if moment, he fearlessly defeats his giant named Goliath, who was armored from head to toe. Oh, did I mention Goliath was over 9' tall and his spear alone weighed somewhere between 150-200 pounds?[40]

Both had the same opportunity to tap into God's power in their what-if moment. However, one encountered defeat, and the other one was victorious. What was the difference between the two?

Notice what they saw. Elijah saw Jezebel as "the problem" (1 Kings 19:3). David never regarded Goliath *as a problem*; rather he concluded, "Goliath, *you have a problem*!" (1 Samuel 17:45-47).

Notice the action taken. When Elijah saw Jezebel's threat, he *ran* for his life (1 Kings 19:3). David *ran* toward Goliath *to take his life* (1 Samuel 17:48).

Notice the result. Elijah ended up in the wilderness (1 Kings 19:4), while David ended up in the King's house (1 Samuel 18:2). The difference between Elijah and David is joy. Elijah opted for fear over joy; David, on the other hand, was delighted because he knew Goliath was going down!

Joy is an energizer and empowers the Christian towards victory. An attitude of joy is vital to winning the battle over the what-ifs. Joy embraces adversity with power and authority, overpowers the emotions, and leads the mind towards sound judgment, leading to victory over the what-if.

What about you? How do you respond when you find yourself surrounded by the hardships of life?

Empowerment through Embracing the Joy Battle Plan:

Reinforce the spirit of joy by studying the principles below. Consider looking up the definitions of each word and the scriptures. Write your takeaway and how you can incorporate these principles as you live out God's power in the face of adversity.

- **Rejoice** <u>as soon as</u> we encounter the trial. – Psalms 30:1; James 1:2; 1 Thess 5:18
- **Reject** thoughts that exalt themselves over the knowledge of Christ. – Gen 6:5; Psalms 10:4; Psalms 94:11; Psalms 139:23-24; 2 Corinth 10:5
- **Remember** God's faithfulness in the past. – Lamentations 3:21-22
- **Replace** thoughts with biblical thinking (God's Word). Psalms 19:14; Psalms 119:113-114; Prov 12:5; Prov 15:26; Prov 16:3; Isa 55:7-8
- **Rely** on God's power and resources (Holy Spirit). – John 14:16-17; John 14:26; John 15:26
- **Realize** the greater work taking place within rather than without. – Eph 3:20; Phil 2:13; Col 1:29

- **Recognize** who is speaking. – Psalms 29:4; Psalms 55:3; Psalms 95:7-8; John 10:27
- **Relish** in victory over the enemy. – 1 Corinthians 15:57; 1 John 5:4; Rev 12:11; Rev 15:2

Chapter 12
Empowered over Discouragement

"The remedy for discouragement is the
Word of God. When you feed your heart and
mind with its truth, you regain your
perspective and find renewed strength."[41]
—Warren Wiersbe

One definition of discouragement is "dispirited." A feeling of discouragement, unhappiness, lack of confidence or enthusiasm, or apathy. It's a malicious mindset that weighs heavily on our spirit. Other words that describe this attitude are disheartened, dejected, or downhearted.[42] My experience with discouragement has been exhausting. I battled for months while preparing to celebrate twenty years of ministry. My feeling of inadequacy, stemming from the realization that I had not made a difference or done anything significant in twenty years, led to my discouragement. I convinced myself that *all* the hard work, *all* the prayers, pushing through fatigue, and *everything* I did was in vain, that I had accomplished *nothing*. (Notice the extremes of discouragement, ALL, EVERTHING, NOTHING). I wanted to quit. Retire. And do something else. I wasn't sure what "something else" entailed, but it did not include ministry.

I realized the depressing thoughts were not from God, who is my number one cheerleader. I recognized this wasn't His method as God doesn't lead us to dead ends. I was aware that the voices in my head were the enemy's attempt to move me off God's chosen path. I felt powerless, but I wasn't. Eventually, I overcame the "deadly D's" and here I am today, still in ministry and still pressing forward for the cause of Christ.

Many factors can trigger discouragement: fatigue, fear of failure, an overwhelming to-do list, or negative influences either in the mind or from others. Its purpose is to tempt you to quit or frustrate your progress. Did you know it's possible to make a living as a professional frustrater? At least this was one of the "services" offered for hire in biblical days. When the adversaries of Judah and Benjamin heard the exiles had returned and were rebuilding the Temple, they tried to interrupt their progress. Their first tactic was to ask them to "join them." Zerubbabel saw through their lies and promptly declined. Since their first attempt failed, they "hired counselors against them to frustrate their purpose all the days of Cyrus, king of Persia, even until the reign of Darius, king of Persia" (Ezra 4:5), which was a period of fourteen years.

The adversary is persistent and will taunt the Christian until it achieves its goal. What-if moments are filled with setbacks, roadblocks, detours, and dead ends. If we don't stop discouragement, it will stop us. It's crucial to stay vigilant about its dangers and prepare for its inevitable attack. The world offers many ways to escape the pains of despair, depression, and despondency. But Jesus Christ is our encourager and will stabilize your journey as you allow the light of His Word to shine into whatever difficulty you are facing.

I promise you that even when you feel downhearted, God's Word will lift your spirits and get you back on track. Keep in mind, this is a process, not an overnight fix. Elijah's experiences teach us that discouragement is a bump in the road, not a dead end. Even the strongest of saints can become discouraged. God worked extraordinary miracles through Israel's prophet Elijah. He was a man of like nature as we are, yet he prophesied a three-year drought, prayed fire down from heaven, defeated 450 prophets of Baal, and confronted the evil King Ahab without flinching. However, after these miraculous victories, we don't find Elijah rejoicing on the mountaintop; instead, we find him fleeing to Rock Bottom Valley.

How did he get there? Ahab told his wife, Jezebel, everything Elijah had done, including how he killed all the prophets. "Jezebel was enraged about the death of her prophets because they told her everything she wanted to hear, prophesying her future of power and glory." She then issued a threat to take Elijah's life. Ahab told Jezebel all that Elijah had done—how he killed with the sword all the men who spoke for Baal. Then Jezebel sent a message to Elijah, saying, "So may the gods do to me and even more, if I don't make your life as the life of one of them by this time tomorrow." Elijah was afraid. He got up and ran for his life.

When he reached Beersheba in Judah, he left his servant there. Then he traveled a day into the desert, sat down under a juniper tree, and asked to die, saying, "It is enough now, O Lord. Take my life. For I'm no better than my fathers" (1 Kings 19:1-4 NIV). Out of fear,

Elijah ran for his life (1 Kings 19:3). Previously, Elijah had clearly demonstrated that Jezebel's god was weak, but her threat caused him to shift from being "unstoppable" to feeling that "it's enough; now, O Lord, take away my life," as he lamented. "I am not better than my fathers" (1 Kings 19:4). What led to his decline? How did Elijah transition from being a victor to becoming a victim?

1. **Issues that led to Elijah's downfall:**

   • **Elijah averted his gaze from the Lord.** When Jezebel issued a death threat, Elijah *saw* Jezebel's warning as a cause for alarm, and he fled for his life. Elijah failed to keep his eyes on God, his defender. Hebrews 12:2 admonishes the Christian to "look away [from all that will distract] and look to Jesus, Who is the Leader and Source of our faith" (Hebrews 12:2 AMP).

   • **Elijah let fear take precedence over faith.** Elijah had a choice—faith over fear. When Elijah surrendered to the spirit of fear, he gave it the power to move him off God's chosen path. Psalm 56:3 reminded us to trust God even when we're afraid. Jezebel was controlling, vicious, and cunning, but she was no match for the God of Israel.

2. **The dangers of discouragement:**

- **The urge to quit.** Galatians 6:9 warns about becoming weary [spiritless in our minds]. When this happens, we'll want to quit.

- **Absence of enthusiasm.** Elijah lost his passion for God's greatness. When we lose our passion, we'll lose the drive to persist. "It is enough," Elijah informed God. "I'm done!" "Through!" "Finished!" In his book, *Be Yourself: Discover the Life You Were Meant to Live*, author John Mason has much to say about the energetic force of passion. He said, "God put inside each person the potential to be passionate. One person with passion makes a greater impact than the passive force of ninety-nine who are only interested... The atmosphere of your life changes drastically when you add enthusiasm.... Ignore what you are passionate about, and you ignore one of the greatest potentials God has put inside you."[43]

- **Foolish Prayer Requests.** When we yield to discouragement, we're in danger of making unwise prayer requests or not praying. 1 Thessalonians 5:17 teaches us to "Pray without ceasing." Why? Because life's battles never end. Do you think Elijah's journey would've been different had he invited God into his situation or asked for courage to face Jezebel?

- **Insensitivity to God's intervention.** Scriptures tell us Elijah went a day's journey into the wilderness. Found a juniper tree, sat down, asked God to take his life, and went to sleep. An angel brought fresh bread and water, waking him up for dinner. He ate and drank and nonchalantly went back to sleep. As if having an angel bring food was an everyday occurrence. To Elijah's defense, however, God used ravens to bring him food … so perhaps the angel's appearance wasn't as shocking as we might think. God sent nourishment, yet there's no sign of thankfulness or awe about the miracle. When we're depressed, our hearts become dull to God's magnificence. Psalm 145:5 said, *"I will meditate on the glorious* *splendor of Your majesty, And on Your wondrous works.* "We're in a dangerous place spiritually when we're no longer impressed by God's miracles. Spiritual dryness will lead to decay. Do you want to "keep your spirits up?" Never lose the amazement over God's majesty.

3. **The delights of discouragement**

- **God's abiding presence.** Elijah fled a day's journey into the wilderness, yet God's presence met him where he was. Psalm 139:7 "Whither shall I go from thy spirit? or whither shall I flee from thy presence?"

- **The presence of God's love.** Elijah beat himself up with regret and was drained physically, mentally, and spiritually. He didn't need a 3-point sermon to get him back on track. Instead, he needed God's loving, kind, and gentle voice of affirmation. And that is exactly what he received. Notice when God posed the question, "What doest thou here, Elijah" (1 Kings 19:9).

- **Insightful teachings on God's authority.** I often wondered why God allowed the great and strong wind, powerful enough to knock over rocks, followed by an earthquake and fire. Yet God wasn't in any of these. One reason is that the god that Israel worshiped was the god over nature; their perception was that all aspects of life were under its control. Had the gods been in charge, the wind, earthquake, or fire would have destroyed Elijah. God reminded Elijah that He was Ruler over all things, and nothing could harm him without going against God's authority.

- **No condemnation.** There is no evidence that God condemned Elijah for running away. Instead, we see God's compassion and mercies, which fail not. "It is of the LORD'S mercies that we are not consumed, because his compassions fail not" (Lamentations 3:22).

- **Purpose after discouragement.** God didn't discuss Jezebel or the events that led to Elijah's downfall. He simply hands Elijah a to-do list, as a reminder that failure wasn't final, he was still useful, and his work wasn't finished.

- **Empowerment over discouragement.** – 1 Kings 19:19 told us, "So he departed from there…" Yes, Elijah was discouraged, depressed, and regarded life as no longer worth living. But God, in His mercy and grace, walked with him through the darkness to the other side. God understands when His children get discouraged. He'll pick us up and gently get us back on track.

4. **How discouragement can be avoided.**

- **Discern the root.** Following 40 days in the wilderness, God asked Elijah, "What doest thou here, Elijah? When you're in the pit of despair, ask yourself, "What am I doing here?" "How did I get here?" Go back and figure out where you took the wrong turn. And take the steps to get back on track. This could include godly counsel or a good, old-fashioned prayer meeting with God as you pour out your heart to him. (See more on prayer and isolation in the following two points.)

- **Remember to "always pray and not faint."** (Luke 18:1). The only recorded prayer Elijah prayed was asking God to take his life. (Praise the Lord for unanswered prayer!) The outcome may have been different had Elijah at once taken his need to the Lord. After all, he knew God heard his prayers, and he had already seen God perform many miracles. Luke 18:1 warns the Christian to pray and not faint. Faint means to be utterly spiritless, to be wearied out, exhausted. One of my former pastors, Dr. Homer G. Lindsay, Jr., taught, "When you feel least like praying is when you need to pray the most." Elijah could have avoided a lot of heartache if he had "taken his need to the Lord in prayer."

- **Ask for help from others.** Elijah "…and left his servant there. But he himself went a day's journey into the wilderness…" (1 Kings 19:3-4). Hebrews 10:25 cautions the Christian about forsaking the assembling of ourselves. "Not forsaking the assembling of ourselves together, as the manner of some is; but exhorting one another: and so much the more, as ye see the day approaching." Ecclesiastes 4:9-10 reminded us that two are better than one. If one falls, the other will be there to lift him up. "Two *are* better than one; because they have a good reward for their labor. For if they fall, the one will lift up his fellow: but woe to him that is alone when he falleth; for he hath not another to help him up." Although we're tempted to hide when we're feeling mentally weak or spiritually depleted (after all, we want to be viewed as super-spiritual saints), it's possible we need to reach out for help. In Elijah's situation, the servant could have encouraged Elijah by reminding him that Jezebel was no threat or by highlighting the miracles and victory he had just won. When feeling discouraged, the last recourse shouldn't be "leave others behind and go it alone." In fact, we need to surround ourselves with those who lift us spiritually. There are times we need to be alone. In the New Testament, we find Jesus alone in the mountains praying, such as in Luke 9:18. Alone time isn't necessarily bad. However, if we are feeling discouraged and depressed, we should seek help, not flee and hide.

Empowerment through Discouragement Battle Plan:

Embrace the power of faith. You're stronger than you realize. The same power that raised Jesus from the dead lives in you. Just as we build strength in muscles through movement, develop your faith through practice.

Embrace the power of purpose. You were created intentionally, with a purpose. God has placed His plans within you. Elijah was made to overcome a formidable opponent, and so are you.

Embrace the power of weakness. Regarding his thorn as a weakness, Paul asked God three times to remove it. Scripture did not specify Paul's thorn, but the implication is that Paul thought the thorn made him weak. God reminded him, "His power was made perfect in weakness" (2 Corinthians 12:9).

Recognize your weakness and seek out God's power made available through them. Two important lessons we learn from Elijah's Rock Bottom experience: Life's difficulties may take us down, but not out. And no matter how far down we go, we will never fall from God's grace! Where has your what-if moment taken you? On the Top of the Mountain or in Rock Bottom Valley? No matter where you are, God is there. Stay strong. He'll lift you and establish your goings.

Chapter 13
Empowered in our Mess

"I am sorry for the Christian who has not
something in his circumstances he wishes
was not there."[44]
—Oswald Chambers

George Mueller said,

"In a thousand trials, it's not just five hundred
that work for our good, but nine hundred and
ninety-nine-plus one!" The scripture, "God
planned good to come out of it...," means
that no disaster, disease, or delay can keep
Him from turning it into something
worthwhile. Understanding that God forgives
your past, knows your present, and planned
your future, enables you to walk in
confidence knowing nothing can ever happen
to you beyond the scope of His grace and
redemption."[45]

I don't know about you, but my year has been a
mess; I feel as if I've been on a roller coaster. More
often than I want to admit, a frequent prayer of mine
has been, "Lord, I'm a mess." Even though it's been a

challenging year, God used the messy what-ifs to heighten my ability to share His truths while writing this book. I've felt His presence as He assured me, He knows my needs and, even in a mess, He's with me every step. Is there a message in our mess? As we search for answers, we'll discover precious jewels scattered throughout life's messy pathway. God's purpose is to grow us through the what-ifs so others will see more of Him in our lives.

Often, we regard God as the 911 operator. Someone to contact when our lives are in disorder. We're inclined to *use* God rather than submit to His leadership so that we're helpful in Him.

When we're hurting, we often beg, "God, make it better." God responds, "My goal is to make you better." When we're clueless about how to handle a situation, we cry, "God, please fix this!" Shaking His head, God affirms, "I'm more interested in fixing you." In desperation, we shout, "God, please hurry and get me through this hard season." In His still small voice, He explains, "Unless the seed remains in the dark, damp soil, it won't develop and grow. The same is true for you; if I rush you through this time of sorrow, you will miss the joys of growing in wisdom and grace."

Knowing God works in the messy seasons of life sharpens our senses and broadens our understanding regarding the value of suffering. In our mess, like Job, we're not aware how God is using the mess as a learning tool. This was Job's experience. In one day, he lost his property and all ten of his children. As if that wasn't enough to deal with, shortly thereafter, Satan attacked his health by striking him "with boils from the sole of his foot unto his crown" (Job 2:6). In a short time, Job went from the richest man in the world, "to sitting among the ashes" (Job 3:8). And to add to the messiness, three friends showed up "to set him straight." After enduring immense suffering, anguish of his soul, oppression, weariness, penetrating grief, and miserable comforters (Job 16:1), Job experienced the highs and lows of perseverance, which ultimately led to a breakthrough when his spiritual vision of God cleared. "I had heard of You [only] by the hearing of the ear, But now my [spiritual] eye sees You" (Job 42:5 AMP).

A question someone may ask is: What if I fail in my what-if moment? As we learn how to win the war over *what-ifs*, it's important to remember that mistakes are unavoidable and a valuable part of the journey. Without slipups, our knowledge would remain limited. "Successful people believe mistakes are just feedback. You can learn something from everything." (John Mason)

As the apostle Peter learned, with the mess often comes regret. Regret's penalty is disturbing; it's a feeling of sorrow, loss, and remorse. It's universal and no respecter of people. It involves blaming ourselves for a bad outcome. The what-if tortures our spirits, causing desires for revisions. Certain individuals can progress. Others anguish over them throughout the course of their lives.

God ordained the Apostle Peter as leader of the first church (Matthew 16:18). Peter learned the impact of a messy *what-if* the hard way. Little did he realize the path to being used mightily by God would be paved with unwise choices. However, as we will observe through Peter's experience, even when we fail, God's grace empowers us to move beyond the failure and back on the road to success. Peter missed the opportunity to infuse God's power in his what-if moment when he failed to manage effectively God's message, his mouth, his "moment", and his mind. Because Peter placed confidence in himself rather than Jesus' wisdom, he failed by not heeding God's message (Luke 22:31-34).

Managing the mouth wasn't one of Peter's strong traits. Even after Jesus predicted Peter would deny Him, Peter adamantly declared his loyalty. "Peter said unto him, Though I should die with thee, yet will I not deny thee. Likewise, also said all the disciples" (Matthew 26:35).

Lingering around the fire contributed to Peter's mismanagement of his moment when he denied Jesus three times. Peter tried unsuccessfully to manage his mind when fear won over faith. As soon as the words of denial were out of Peter's mouth, the agony of his actions hurled him into the horrifying pit of hopelessness. Thankfully, this was short-lived. Jesus wasn't surprised by Peter's denial; He had predicted it.

Jesus cushioned Peter's fall with prayer. Notice, Jesus didn't pray that Peter wouldn't fall; instead, He prayed his faith wouldn't fail (Luke 22:32).

Jesus didn't regard Peter's denial as the end of Peter's ministry. He knew Peter's failure was a necessary stepping-stone towards his success (Luke 22:32b). Note, Jesus didn't say to Peter, "if" thou art converted, but "when." We have a choice. We can either allow our mistakes to *define us* or *refine us*. Perhaps you are in the trenches of regret.

It's time to R-E-L-E-A S-E it and allow God's forgiveness and grace to elevate your confidence and fortify your course. The seven methods of release describe actions we can take towards freedom from the bondage of regret.

- **R**EFUSE to allow destructive thoughts to dwell in our minds by bringing every thought captive to the obedience of Christ (2 Corinthians 10:5).
- **E**MBRACE responsibility for our choices. The process towards freedom mandates owning up to the fact that the decision made was ours (Psalm 51:4).

- **L**ET GO of past mistakes (Psalm 51:3). For example, writing a letter or recording the experience, seeking forgiveness, or granting ourselves the freedom to make mistakes, making amends, i.e., paying back an unpaid debt.

- **E**XAMINE the reason for the mistake or wrong choice. What did we learn, and how can we apply this knowledge as we move forward? (Psalm 51:6).

- **A**CCEPT "it-is-what-it-is". It is impossible to undo any action, no matter how much we agonize or fret. A word spoken cannot be taken back, and an act cannot be reversed. Our mistake will not vanish with the wave of a wand. Acknowledge the slip-up and look forward to brighter days (Philippians 3:13a).

- Recognize the **S**OURCE of spirit-depleting thoughts. Discern which spirit is speaking by measuring our thoughts against God's Word.

- **E**XPECT to make more mistakes; it's a specific part of growing into the image of Christ.

Have you ever made a mistake or an unwise choice? The fact that you failed is proof that you're moving. Progress is stalled when we stop learning. "Failure and mistakes can be a bridge, not a barricade to success."[46] It is not how many days we live, it's how we live our days. Regret is unavoidable. Don't relive it—Release it into God's Hands and patiently wait as He works all things together for good.

Winning the war over the what-if moments requires giving yourself grace. The road to success is lined with many mistakes and regrets. The next time you find yourself in the pit of shame, say, "I didn't come this far to fail." Reach out and grasp God's rope of hope, pull yourself up, and keep going… until Jesus comes.

Empowerment through our Mess Battle Plan:

Embrace the power of mistakes. Don't hide them; instead, expose them to discover their value and learn for future efforts.

Embrace the power of teachability. A teachable attitude opens the door to growth.

Embrace the power of grace. How often do we criticize ourselves for past mistakes? Give yourself grace. Allow yourself to fail and rest in the knowledge that it's all part of getting closer to success.

How can embracing our mess lead to a sense of empowerment? In what ways can recognizing the value in our failures transform our approach to challenges? What lessons have I gained from my recent mistakes? How can I cultivate a more teachable attitude? In what areas of my life do I need to extend more grace?

Today, choose to see your mess as a stepping stone. Share one lesson you've learned from a mistake with someone who needs encouragement. Embrace your journey, imperfections and all, and move forward with confidence.

Chapter 14
Empowered to Finish

"We'll be judged by what we finish, not
what we start."
—John Mason[47]

The above quote makes me cringe; however, it's essential to face the truth of these words. Others will remember not what we start, but what we finish. I faced a critical decision in my what-if moment last year when my husband and I celebrated twenty years of ministry. Reaching this milestone should have brought elation and a feeling of accomplishment. But for me, it was the opposite. I battled thoughts of quitting as my team, filled with excitement and enthusiasm, worked tirelessly to plan an elaborate celebration. All year, I fought voices in my head, mocking me with questions such as "What have you accomplished in twenty years?" "Has your work touched others' lives?" "Have you had an impact?"

The turning point of my *what-if* scenario came after our highly successful retreat. My husband and I had a choice—continue the ministry or retire. After much prayer and soul-searching, we sensed God wasn't closing the door to our ministry and began planning for the following year's events. From my recent dilemma about whether to retire or go forward, I settled on next year's retreat's theme: Don't give up! Rise up! And turn your adversity into advancement.

What empowers us to overcome the *what-ifs*? I believe overcoming is achieved by finishing strong with faith. "For whosoever is born of God overcometh the world: and this is the victory that overcometh the world, [even] our faith" (1 John 5:4).

Why do Christians live in defeat? I believe one reason is that we have an actual enemy who is "defeated" each time a glorious victory is won in our lives, and he does not like it! Every time we refuse to give in to our doubts, fears, discouragement, and we step out in faith … expecting God to come through … Satan is threatened and fights back with vengeance.

Webster defines victory as a success or triumph over an enemy in battle or war. The opposite of victory is defeat. When a Christian learns and applies the secret of living the victorious life, then the opponent, the devil, is beaten down. He takes the Christian faith personally and is threatened by a Christian living the victorious life.

The unknown author of How to Live the Victorious Life has this to say about the teachings on Victory:

> "Satan will do his utmost to cloud our mind. He will bring all sorts of doubts and difficulties to light. Why is this? Because he is eager to prevent us from gaining Victory! Believe me, the devil does not mind our being "religious," and he does not mind how much powerless work we attempt so long as we fall short of the Victorious life. As long as we go to the world for our pleasures, and as long as we fall into the usual sins of respectable people, the more we "attempt" for Christ the more the devil is pleased. He simply revels in seeing defeated, worldly Christians desperately busy for Christ. But the devil will do his level best to discredit Victorious Life teaching and to keep you from even seeking to understand it."[48]

I experienced the "cloudiness" and confusion while writing this book. But faith pulled me through. Not faith in myself, but faith in a God who is big enough to write a book. After all, He authored the Bible, and it's been around for thousands of years.

Fuel your spirit with *a word* from God. "Thy word is a lamp unto my feet, and a light unto my path" (Psalm 119:105). "This is my comfort in my affliction: for thy word hath quickened me" (Psalm 119:50).

As a young Christian, I was taught to read God's word until "I got a word from Him." Some days it takes longer than others. Just as a vehicle cannot operate without fuel, neither can we finish unless we fuel our souls daily.

Plug into God's power with prayer. "Evening, and morning, and at noon, will I pray, and cry aloud: and he shall hear my voice" (Psalm 55:17). Prayer is a privilege; it's powerful and pertinent to winning the war over the *what-ifs*. Without prayer, we won't be victorious. Do you find it difficult to pray? One reason is that Satan would have us think God won't hear our prayers unless our lives are flawless. The lives of four individuals found in Scripture proved otherwise. Their lives were not perfect, yet in their time of need, God heard and answered their request.

Samson was at the end of his ministry and had failed God. Jonah was amid rebellion. Peter was fearful. And the thief on the cross had made wrong choices. Indeed, their prayers would not be heard. Still, God answered them with tenderness and compassion. What lessons do Samson, Jonah, Peter, and the thief on the cross teach?

In the last moments of his life, God gave Samson the strength to conquer the Philistines, and "So the dead he slew at his death were more than they which he slew in his life" (Judges 16:30).

Jonah ended up in the fish's belly because of disobedience. When he cried "out of his affliction," God "heard him out of the belly of hell" and delivered him from the fish's belly.

Peter took his eyes off Jesus and allowed fear rather than faith to rule in his heart. Yet, when he cried out, Jesus immediately stretched out a hand and caught him.

The thief, in his last hours on earth, asked Jesus, "… Lord, remember me when thou comest into thy kingdom. And Jesus said unto him, Verily I say unto thee, Today shalt thou be with me in paradise." What if the thief had not prayed? The window of his opportunity would have been lost.

Each of these men was in great trouble; they were in a mess. There wasn't time to use the ACTS formula or "the 12 steps towards an effective prayer life." Yet, we see the LORD responded to the cry of their heart just when they needed Him the most.

Prayer is not an attitude attained, but an attitude maintained and is essential as we overcome in the what-if moments.

Intensify your strength by giving God your weakness. "And he said unto me, My grace is sufficient for thee: for my strength is made perfect in weakness. Most gladly therefore will I rather glory in my infirmities, that the power of Christ may rest upon me. (2 Corinthians 12:9). The identity of Paul's thorn isn't disclosed; however, Paul considered that it weakened his ability to serve the Lord effectively. God reminded Paul that it was because of his thorn (his weakness) that the pathway was opened for God's strength.

I've experienced God's power manifested in my weakness time and time again. Many times, when my energy was depleted, I felt as if I couldn't take another step. The day before my events, the fatigue monster would overwhelm me. But I'd get through the day and back up the next morning, often without a whole night's rest. While teaching or ministering to my ladies, I'd experience a supernatural power surge. Why? Because of my weakness, God's grace made me strong.

Fannie Crosby has written many hymns that have strengthened Christians through the years. Blinded at a young age, she learned the sufficiency of God's power through her physical limitations. She once said, "If I had not lost my sight, I could not have written these hymns."[49] Is your strength gone? Let God take over, and you'll be soaring like an eagle again in no time.

Electrify the race with patience. "Behold, we count them happy which endure. Ye have heard of the patience of Job, and have seen the end of the Lord; that the Lord is very pitiful, and of tender mercy" (James 5:11). Patience is the ability to bear trials without grumbling. It is staying cheerful (or hopeful) as we endure the trials of life. Patience gives the strength to "wait patiently." It stays under the load until the task is completed. Some things in life we "just have to go through." We'd rather not, and if possible, would choose a different path. But without the trial, there would be no patience. The trying of our faith "works" patience" (James 1:1-4). Patience is our friend, not our enemy, and empowers us to be finishers.

Revitalize your energy by waiting on the Lord. "But they that wait upon the Lord shall renew their strength; they shall mount up with wings as eagles; they shall run, and not be weary; and they shall walk, and not faint" (Isaiah 40:31). Only as we choose to wait on the Lord is our strength renewed. One meaning of the word "renew" is "revitalize" or "reawaken."[50] Have you been there, spiritless, without the strength to move? But as you "waited on the Lord", you felt the fresh waters of His grace springing forth, energizing and enabling you to ascend above your weariness?

Author Millie Hamm reminds us that:

> "Often the burdens of life press upon us so heavily we feel we cannot carry them any longer. We ask God to remove them, but His plan is to use them to develop wing power in our lives." In other words, waiting on HIM gives the quiet confidence of His presence upholding us moment by moment."[51]

Author Andrew Murray reassures us that:

> "Waiting always involves the character of our thoughts of the one on whom we wait. Our waiting on God will depend on our faith in who He is. In our text, we have the close of a passage in which God reveals Himself as the everlasting and almighty One. It is as that revelation enters our soul that the waiting becomes the spontaneous expression of what we know Him to be – a God altogether worthy to be waiting upon."[52]

Boost your journey with praise and thanksgiving. "Let us come before his presence with thanksgiving and make a joyful noise unto him with psalms" (Psalm 95:2). When your what-if moment overwhelms you, stop and take an "in everything give thanks" break.

Rejuvenate your spirit by counting your blessings, not your troubles.

Energize your spirit with joy. "They that sow in tears shall reap in joy" (Psalm 126:5). When Jesus was on the cross, it was "*the joy* that was set before Him" that enabled Him to endure the cross (Hebrews 12:2). Joy is an attitude that keeps us motivated until the task is done.

Enhance your mind with alertness. "So prepare your minds for action, be completely sober [in spirit—steadfast, self-disciplined, spiritually and morally alert], fix your hope completely on the grace [of God] that is coming to you when Jesus Christ is revealed," (1 Peter 1:13 AMP).

A Christian with a sloppy/sluggish mindset will fizzle out long before they reach the finish line. As Christians, we must guard our thoughts and the intent of the heart. Proverbs 4:23 says, Keep thy heart with all diligence; for out of it are the issues [source] of life.

Fire up with God's Grace. "And God is able to make all grace abound toward you; that ye, always having all sufficiency in all things, may abound to every good work" (2 Cor 9:8). Only by God's grace are we able to endure the hardships and persevere to the end. We have an enemy that works diligently to quench the fire of God's grace, but we have the Holy Spirit who quenches his efforts and keeps us going until we cross the finish line. God's grace. As God empowers you to win the war over the *what-ifs,* and you cross the finish line, and the observers interview you with this question, "Why were you able to go the distance?"

With confidence, you can say, "Because of the oil of His grace." "For by grace are ye saved through faith; and that not of yourselves: it is the gift of God" (Ephesians 2:8).

Don't cross the finish line alone. Everyone you meet is battling what-if moments. As I conclude this book, I want to close with a reminder: "We're all in this together." I've gained victory over my *what-ifs* because of the people God placed in my life: my husband, my family, my friends. Everyone has played an essential role in encouraging me and cheering for me as I pushed towards the finish line. I cannot thank God enough for everyone He has placed in my path. The delightful story about nine contestants running the race is a reminder that it's not simply crossing the finish line; rather, it's all about crossing the finish line together.

A few years ago, at the Seattle Special Olympics, nine contestants, all physically or mentally disabled, assembled at the starting line for the 100-yard dash. At the gun, they all started out, not exactly in a dash, but with a relish to run the race to the finish and win. All except one little boy who stumbled on the asphalt, tumbled over a couple of times, and began to cry.

The other eight heard the boy cry, slowed down, and looked behind them. Then they turned around and went back, all eight of them. One girl bent down and kissed him and said, "this will make it better." Then all nine linked arms and walked together to the finish line.

Everyone in the stadium stood, and the cheering went on for several minutes. People who were there are still telling the story. Why? Because deep down we know this one thing: What matters in life is more than winning for ourselves. It is helping others win, even if it means slowing down and changing our course.[53]

Never forget, you're a winner. You're an overcomer. And there isn't one what-if moment that God cannot empower you to overcome. Don't give up! Rise up! And enjoy the rewards of victory.

"Thanks *be* unto God for his unspeakable gift" (2 Corinthians 9:15).

Empowerment through Finishing Battle Plan:

Embrace the power to finish. If you tend to stop short of your goals, I suggest several books that helped me shorten my undone pile. Let Go of Whatever Holds You Back by John Mason and What's Really Holding You Back? Closing the Gap Between Where You Are and Where You Want to Be by Valorie Burton.

Embrace the power of choice. John Mason reminded us, "Your destiny is not a matter of chance; it's a matter of choice. Many people have the right aims in life—they just never get around to pulling the trigger." What choices can you make today that will move you closer to your goals?

Embrace the power of persistence. In his book, Be Yourself: Discover the Life You Were Meant to Live, John Mason writes, "All progress is due to those who weren't satisfied to let well enough alone. The difference between ordinary and extraordinary is that little extra." "The deeper we go in God, the deeper He goes in us." I believe in you. You have what it takes—give it your best. Tap into your God-given power to go the distance. Soon enough, you'll be crossing that finish line, hands raised, thanking God for your strength to persevere.

To finish strong, be sure to:

1. **Clarify Your Goal:** Define precisely what finishing looks like for you. Is it completing a project, overcoming a challenge, or reaching a personal milestone?

2. **Strengthen Your Resolve:** Remind yourself of your why. Recall the power of persistence and the deep inner strength you possess.

3. **Prepare for Obstacles:** Anticipate doubts and setbacks. How will you prepare to push past these barriers?

4. **Take Consistent Action:** Break your goal into manageable steps. What is the next small step you can take today?

5. **Seek Support:** Who can encourage you on this journey? Remember, perseverance is a collective effort.

6. **Celebrate Progress:** Recognize every victory along the way. How will you reward yourself?

7. Visualize Success: Picture yourself crossing the finish line with pride. Feel the gratitude and joy.

8. Are you ready to commit to your finish line today? Will you step up, push through, and claim your victory?

Remember, your perseverance is a testament to your strength, faith, and unwavering spirit. Keep going—your victory awaits on the other side.

References

1. Charles Spurgeon, https://www.azquotes.com/citation/quote/874561

2. Charles E. Cowman, *Streams in the Desert,* (Zondervan Corporation, 1996), 370

3. Charles Spurgeon, https://www.azquotes.com/citation/quote/280421

4. Pastor Chris Winford, FBC Brunswick, GA

5. Ralph Waldo Emerson, https://www.azquotes.com/citation/quote/609628

6. https://www.merriam-webster.com/dictionary/sluggishness

7. https://www.merriam-webster.com/dictionary/zealous

8. Obtained from internet: https://www.desiringgod.org/articles/lay-aside-the-weight-of-sluggishness, using with permission via email dated August 9, 2025 from Desiring God permissions@desiringgod.org

9. https://www.dictionary.com/browse/tenacity

10. https://www.wordforyou.com/, March 7, 2022, 8

11. https://www.wordforyou.com/, March 8, 2022, 8

12. Jon Walker, *Growing with Purpose*, (Zondervan, 2009), 15

13. https://biblejesus.com/others-charles-d-meigs/, accessed September 2, 2025

14. John Mason, *Be Yourself: Discover the Life You Were Meant to Live,* (Baker Publishing Group, 2011), 115-116

15. Ralph Waldo Emerson, https://www.azquotes.com/author/4490-Ralph_Waldo_Emerson

16. https://www.merriam-webster.com/dictionary/empowered

17. Chuck Swindoll, *Victory, a Winning Game Plan for Life*, (W Pub Group, 1984), 57-59

18. Millie Stamm, *Be Still and Know* (Zondervan Publishing House, 1978), September 12

19. Millie Stamm, *Be Still and Know* (Zondervan Publishing House 1978), September 12

20. Jentezen Franklin, *Believe That You Can: It's Time to Make It Happen* (Charisma House, 2008), 101

21. *Promises from God for Today*, (CTA Inc., 2020), Motivational cards.

22. Google Search, Dictionary, search.yahoo.com

23. Andrew Murray, https://www.liveatthewell.org/quotes-from-andrew-murray.html, September 15

24. Elizabeth Elliot, https://www.azquotes.com/author/17940-Elisabeth_Elliot/tag/waiting

25. Oswald Chambers, *My Utmost for His Highest,* (Discovery House Publishers, 2010), 43

26. Charles Stanley, https://quotefancy.com/quote/2247670/Charles-F-Stanley-When-you-face-a-mountain-in-yourlife-you-have-a-choice-be-overwhelmed

27. Tim LaHaye, *The Battle for the Mind,* (Fleming H. Revell, 1980), 18-19

28. Helen Grace Lescheid, *Daily Guideposts,* (Guideposts, 2009), 14.

29. Millie Stamm, *Be Still and Know* (Zondervan Publishing House, 1978), January 1.

30. www.wordforyou.com, *The Word for You Today,* Abraham (Part 3), July 11

31. Ibid.

32. Charles E. Cowman, *Streams in the Desert*, Copyright © 1996 by The Zondervan Corporation, July 9, page 209.

33. Charles R Swindoll, *Three Steps Forward Two Steps Back: Persevering through Pressure,* (Bantam Books, 1980), 83

34. Charles R. Swindoll, *Three Steps Forward Two Steps Back, Persevering through Pressure,* (Bantam Books, 1980) 76

35. www.wordforyoutoday.com, *Change Your Self-Talk*, March 5

36. Jospeh Stowell, *When the Going Gets Tough*, Discovery Series Bible Study, (Discovery House Publishers, 2012), 44

37. Joseph Stowell, *When the Going Gets Tough*, Discovery Series Bible Study (Discovery House Publishers, 2012), 45

38. Charles F. Stanley, *How to Handle Adversity,* (Thomas Nelson, 1989), 11-12

39. Notes in part from Dr. H.L. Willmington, *Willmington's Guide to the Bible*, (Tyndal House Publishers, Inc., 2011) 511-512

40. https://www.blueletterbible.org/comm/ guzik_david/study-guide/1-samuel/1-samuel-17.cfm?a=253005

41. https://www.bibleportal.com/bible-quote/discouragement-scripture-strength-the-remedy-fordiscouragement-is-the-word-of-god-when-you-feed-your-heart-and-mind-with-its-truth-you

42. Accessed via on September 3, 2025, Google search, search.yahoo.com, Dictionary

43. John Mason, *Be Yourself: Discover the Life You Were Meant to Live,* (Revell, 2014), 18

44. Oswald Chambers, *My Utmost for His Highest*, (Discovery House Publishers, 2010), 101

45. www.wordforyoutoday.com, God Planned Good to Come Out of it, February 25

46. John Mason, *Be Yourself: Discover the Life You Were Meant to Live,* (Revell, 2011), 30

47. John Mason, *Let Go of Whatever Hold You Back*, (Revell, 2012), 16

48. By an Unknown Christian, *How to Live the Victorious Life*, (Zondervan Publishing House, 1971), 7

49. Millie Stamm, *Be Still and Know,* (Zondervan Publishing House, 1978), October 30

50. https://www.wordhippo.com/what-is/another-word-for/renew.html, September 15

51. Millie Stamm, *Be Still and Know,* (Zondervan Publishing House, 1978), May 29

52. Andrew Murray, *Waiting on God: A 31-Day Study*, (Revell, 2018), 81

53. Original Source Unknown, partially true story according to Snopes, Seattle Special Olympics, nine contestants, cited on internet on various websites.

Acknowledgements

First and foremost, I thank God for sending Jesus to die on the cross for my sins. Without Him, I would be nothing. I also thank my family—Will, Christy, Shannon, Little Will, Gabe, Bethany, Mati, Hannah, Skylynn, Savannah, Cillian, and Isaiah—and especially my wonderful husband, Ben, for his love, knowledge, and spiritual guidance. I am grateful to my nieces and nephews for their love and encouragement.

Thanks to Katherine Hutchinson-Hayes for her labor of love, friendship, encouragement, and cheering me on throughout my writing journey. I appreciate Karen Griffin for the many hours on the phone, words of encouragement, and praying with me as we both wrote our books.

To my ministry volunteers, thank you for believing in me and letting me walk on the wings of your prayers. Thanks also to the Bible and BBQ with the Gals for your faithfulness and for cheering me on. To the Kauffmans—Rick, Beebe, and Katy—for your kindness, generosity, and investment in the lives of writers.

Thank you, Mary Sweet, who, after all these years, has never stopped believing in me. To everyone who whispered a prayer and offered words of affirmation—you are a treasure to me. And to my readers, thank you for taking the time to read my book. I pray that you are blessed a hundredfold.

Billie Corley is a writer, speaker, bible teacher, and founder of Billie Corley Ministries and has been in Women's Ministry for over twenty-one years. Her heart's desire can be summed up in her ministry's slogan, "Seeking to Teach, Inspire and Encourage Women Everywhere for Jesus Christ."

Billie's life drastically changed when she surrendered her heart to Jesus Christ in her late twenties. Immediately, she had a burden for ladies' ministry and, after a thirty-one-year career in Corporate America, entered full-time Christian service.

Billie shares her love for God's word through her speaking and writing. When she's not writing, Billie spends time hosting and preparing for her annual women's retreat and monthly bible studies.

Billie is a published author of several articles, both online and in print, through Lighthouse Bible Studies and Dressed in Love Press.

Billie serves with spiritual vigor, joy, and enthusiasm, and welcomes the opportunity to share at your ladies' events.

Billie is a wife, stepmom, grand-mommy, and great-grand-mommy, and lives in south Georgia with her soulmate, Ben, and a cat named Blue.

<u>Connect with Billie Corley:</u>

Facebook: @BillieSueStrawderCorley
Facebook: @BillieCorleyMinistries
Instagram: @billiesuecorley

Check out her website for more information:
www.billiecorley.com

<u>Coming Soon:</u>
Why Flounder When You Can Flourish:
How to Grow Through What You Go Through